A PATCHWORK OF PROGRAMS

FOR WOMEN'S MINISTRIES

A PATCHWORK OF PROGRAMS

FOR WOMEN'S MINISTRIES

NORA BURDETT

KAREN KELLER

Beacon Hill Press of Kansas City
Kansas City, Missouri

ISBN: 083-411-4771

Printed in the United States of America

Cover design: Crandall Vail
Cover art: Tom Shank

10   9   8   7   6   5   4   3   2

Dedication

To Ken Burdett and Sam Keller
—our wonderful husbands—

without whom this project would never have become a reality. We thank you both for the love, confidence, encouragement, and patience you have shown us during this project. You not only have lived through the writing of the book but also have actually survived each program in it as well. For everything from the meals you prepared to the endless hours on the computer, we thank you both—and we love you!

Writing a book is an adventure. To begin with, it is a toy and an amusement. Then it becomes a mistress; then it becomes a tyrant. The last phase is that just as you are about to reconcile to your servitude, you kill the monster and fling him about to the public.

—Winston Churchill

Mr. Churchill, this beast nearly conquered us, but it is far from dead. Therefore, to the public we thrust all the life, fun, experience, and hard work we've had in hopes that they will catch the dragon by the tail and make life the adventure it was meant to be.

—Nora Burdett
Karen Keller

Contents

Foreword

Creative ideas for entertaining, either at home or church, are always in short supply, so this book, *A Patchwork of Programs for Women's Ministries,* is certain to meet a definite need for hostesses whose banquets and parties have become predictable. As experienced seamstresses know, a patchwork takes infinite patience and skill to create; this is true of the ideas in this book as well. The authors, wives of church planters in Australia, have tried out each idea they suggest, either in their own homes or in churches their husbands have founded in Australia.

On Fridays in a suburb of Sydney, Australia, Karen Keller and Nora Burdett met at Nora's house for the weekly writing sessions. Although their physical characteristics are quite different—Nora is tall and blond and Karen is petite and brunette—they are both extremely vivacious, and the sound of their laughter mixed with that of the kookaburras just outside on the patio as the two good friends contemplated the day's activities. Generally, as they have told me, Nora was sent to the back bedroom and the computer while Karen stayed in the kitchen with the materials covering counters and table. Lunchtime was spent reviewing and collaborating, pushing the work aside only to share a cup of tea.

Writing is generally looked upon as a lonely craft, but not the way *these* two did it! They exemplify the truth of Eccles. 4:9—"Two are better than one; because they have a good reward for their labour." This book is truly "good reward" for those "writing Fridays" these American girls spent together in the land down under, and I am certain that their ideas will be well received in both their native land and their adopted country.

Being a teacher at a Bible college may not be financially rewarding, but the delight I feel at this accomplishment by my former students is worth more than mere money. They were exciting students in the classroom, and this endeavor by Nora and Karen is typical of their desire for excellence and their unwillingness to just take the easy way.

—Norma Gillming
Professor of Special Needs in Women's Ministries
Baptist Bible College
Springfield, Mo.

Acknowledgments

Thank you to those whose help made our job just a little easier and a lot more fun:

Bonnie Perry—for giving us a chance

Linda and Gary Goodpastor—for proofreading and computer help

Brenda Murphy—for major proofreading

Lois Marks—for final proofreading

Richard and Kathleen Hester—for the use of your guest room and copy machine

Tommy and Joahna Swaims—for the use of your home and computer

Bob Graham—for the use of your computer and facilities

Fran Roelle—for handling correspondence

Jan Mooney—for help with research

Sue Page—for handling our faxes and mail

Introduction

Successful programs do not just happen. Planning and purpose are vital components in developing any idea. To help you in these areas, we have listed some points to consider before preparing any special program.

1. What is your purpose?
2. What is your theme?
3. When will you have it?
4. Where will you have it?
5. How and when will you promote it?
6. Who will do what?
   a. decorations
   b. program (songs, skits, readings, games, speaker, etc.)
   c. food (cooking, serving, cleaning)
7. How will you finance it?
8. Whom do you need to thank? Honor? Invite?

To receive the fullest benefit or expand the use of this book, be attentive to the following guidelines:

1. Pick and choose ideas that fit into your needs. Be creative and imaginative, original and daring. Most good ideas spring from other good ideas. Use these ideas for banquets, home entertaining, and outreach to neighbors.
2. Enlargements and/or copies may be made from any of our illustrations for use as decorations or handouts.
3. Budgets are an integral part of program planning. If you need to spend more than you have, take heart. It is possible! Several of the decorations were made to be sold. They can either reimburse the budget or help you raise money for a project.
4. See if you can "recycle" your work into a program on another day for senior citizens, young people, children, or an after-church fellowship on Sunday night. Let as many people as possible enjoy your efforts.

PART I

Christmas

Patchwork Christmas
Winter Wonderland
A Victorian Christmas
Beary Merry Christmas
Gifts That Keep On Giving

PATCHWORK CHRISTMAS

Options

Christmas/Ladies'/Couples' Party
Missions Banquet
Neighborhood Outreach

Children's Party
Christmas in July

Decorations

Tables   Cover with white paper. Cut Christmas shapes (trees, wreaths, candy canes, etc.) from Christmas wrapping paper or fabric scraps. Attach to table covering with spray adhesive.

Centerpieces   Potted poinsettias

Program Cover   (See Appendix, Item 1-A.)

Name Tags   (See Appendix, Item 1-B.)

Luminarias (a Mexican tradition)   Said to light the way of the Christ child on Christmas Eve. (See Resources.)

Wall Mural   Glue odd shapes of Christmas paper to long pieces of butcher paper, creating a quilt look. The mural should be large—approximately 3' x 5'. Make the "stitches" around each "patch" with a wide black felt pen. Feature a picture of the Nativity, at least 8" x 10", in the center.

Special Features

Australia

Carols by Candlelight   Because Christmas in Australia comes during the hottest days of summer, there are many outdoor candlelight services called "Carols by Candlelight." People sit on the grass, holding lighted candles, and sing favorite carols.

Plum Pudding Reading   (See Resources.)

England

Caroling   Because Christmas is such a cold time in England, people bundle up to carol. Have a group of people come in and sing carols for you. They may be dressed in wool coats, scarves, gloves, and boots, with cheeks and noses rouged as if they have just come in from the cold.

Skit   "Scrooge and the Night Before Christmas" (See Resources.)

Sweden

St. Lucia's Day   The youngest daughter of the household slips out of bed before the others in the house stir. She wears a long, white dress belted with a scarlet sash and a crown of leaves and tall, white candles. She awakens the family by singing Christmas carols and serves each member coffee and cardamom-flavored buns. This tradition can be modified and used during the program. (See Resources for St. Lucia's Crown.)

Mexico

Piñata Game   Piñatas are earthenware pots, dried but unfired, brilliantly decorated with tissue paper and forming shapes such as fish, stars, donkeys, etc. They are filled with candy. The piñata is suspended by rope so that it can be lowered and raised. Usually children form a circle beneath it. One is blindfolded, placed in the center, and given a stick. He is allowed three tries at breaking the piñata. If he doesn't succeed, others take his place one by one until the piñata is broken. You may want to make your own piñata of papier-mâché or purchase one.

Posada   This is a ceremony depicting the trip of Mary and Joseph to Bethlehem. To improvise this, have two people dress up as Mary and Joseph. They appear and ask if there is room for them. They are turned away by the host/hostess several times during the evening. At last they are invited in for a celebration with food and games.

Denmark

Traditional Danish heart decorations can be made as crafts or used as demonstrations. (See Resources.)

Game

Merry Christmas in Many Languages   (See Resources.)

Cookie Exchange

Instead of the traditional gift exchange, try a cookie exchange. Ask each person to make four dozen cookies, wrapping each dozen individually to exchange with four other people. Have them submit their cookie recipes beforehand. Make them into a recipe book.

Devotional

Christmas Visitor   Reading (See Resources.)

"Babushka"   Traditional Russian folk tales for children and "Papa Panvos' Special Day." Check your local library or bookstore for these titles.

Food

Australia   Australian sausage rolls (See Resources.)

England   English trifle (See Resources.)

Mexico   Bizcochitos (Mexican cookies), Mexican hot chocolate (See Resources.)

Sweden   Swedish meatballs, Swedish tea cakes (See Resources.)

Suggested Schedule

1. Guests arrive through luminaria-decorated entry.
2. Australian carols by candlelight.
3. Plum pudding reading.

4. Briefly explain the posada. Then Mary and Joseph enter and are turned away.
5. English carolers.
6. Scrooge skit.
7. Mary and Joseph enter and are turned away.
8. Sweden's St. Lucia shares her tradition and serves small cardamom buns and coffee.
9. Mexican piñata game
10. Mary and Joseph enter and are turned away.
11. Danish paper heart craft.
12. Game—Merry Christmas in Many Languages.
13. Devotion—Reading/poem.
14. Mary and Joseph enter and are welcomed by all.
15. Refreshments (serve Mary and Joseph first, as honored guests).

RESOURCES

Luminarias

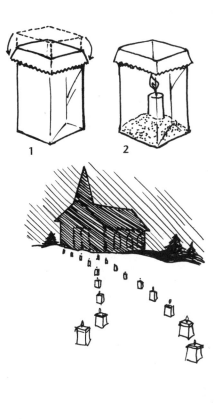

Materials needed:
    Medium-sized flat-bottomed paper grocery bags
    Sand
    Candles

Instructions:
    Fig. 1 Fold down a 2" cuff at the top of bag.
    Fig. 2 Fill the bag with about 3" of sand.
    Place long-burning votive candle in the center of the sand. Place bags on both sides of the walks and/or driveway equal distances apart, leading to the entry.

Plum Pudding Reading

Years ago as the miners and stockmen were "back of beyond" (wherever that is) for months at a time, many found themselves roughing it over Christmas. Here is a story told by Henry Lawson, a much-loved Australian poet, about an unusual Christmas in the outback. Dress someone as a "dinky-di bushman" to read the story. He or she should wear baggy pants, an old shirt, and work boots. Petroleum jelly on the face with dried tea leaves dabbed on gives the look of a heavy growth of whiskers. An Aussie bush hat can be made from a wide-brimmed hat with corks tied around the brim to keep the flies away. This story shows us that it *is* possible to have too much of a good thing.

I got a letter last year from a mate in Western Australia—prospecting the awful desert out beyond White Feather—telling me all about a "perish" he did on plum pudding. He and his mates all camped at the boulder soak [a pond or water hole that is nearly dried up] with some 300 or 400 miles—mostly sand and dust—between them and the nearest grocer's shop.

They ordered a case of mixed canned provisions from Perth to reach them about Christmas. They didn't believe in plum pudding—there are a good many British institutions that bushmen don't believe in—but the cook was a new chum, and he said he'd go home to his mother if he didn't have plum pudding for Christmas, so they ordered a can for him. Meanwhile, they hung out [survived] on kangaroo and damper [bushman's bread] and the knowledge that it couldn't last forever.

It was in a terrible drought, and the kangaroos used to come into the soak for water. They were too weak to run. Later on, when wells were dug, the kangaroos used to commit suicide in them—there was generally a kangaroo in the well in the morning.

The storekeeper packed the case of tinned dog [canned meat], and so on, but by some blunder he or his man put the label on the wrong box, and it went per rail, per coach, per camel, and the last stage per boot, and reached my friend's camp on Christmas Eve, to their great joy. My friend broke the case open by the light of the campfire. "Here, Jack," he said, tossing out a can. "Here's your plum pudding."

He held the next can in his hand a moment longer and read the label twice.

"Why, he's sent *two*," he said, "and I'm sure I only ordered one. Never mind—Jack'll have a tuck-out [large meal]." He held the next can close to the fire and blinked at it hard. "I'll be . . . if he hasn't sent *three* tins of plum pudding. Never mind; we'll manage to scarf some of it between us. You're in luck's way this trip, Jack, and no mistake."

He looked harder still at the fourth can; then he read the labels on the other tins again to see if he'd made a mistake. He didn't tell me what he said then, but a milder mate suggested that the storekeeper had sent half a dozen tins by mistake. But when they reached the seventh tin, the language was not even fit to be written down on a piece of paper up to the magistrate.

The storekeeper had sent them an unbroken case of canned plum pudding, and probably by this time he was wondering what had become of that case of duff [food]. The kangaroos had disappeared by about this time, and my friend tells me that he and his mates had to live for a mortal fortnight on canned plum pudding. They tried it cold, and they tried it boiled. They tried it baked, they tried it fried, and they had it toasted. They had it for breakfast, dinner, and tea. They had nothing else to think, talk, or quarrel about; and they dreamed about it every night, my friend says. It wasn't a joke—it gave them the nightmare and day-horrors.

They tried it with salt. They picked as many of the raisins out as they could and boiled it with salt kangaroo. They tried to make Yorkshire pudding out of it, but it was too rich. My friend was experimenting and trying to discover a simple process for separating the ingredients of plum pudding when a fresh supply of provisions came along. He says he was never so sick of anything in his life, and he has had occasion to be sick of a good many things.

The new chum jackeroo [apprentice] is still alive, but he won't ever eat plum pudding anymore, he says. It cured him of homesickness. He wouldn't eat it even if his bride made it.[1]

---

1. Henry Lawson, "The Ghost of Many Christmases," in Russ Tyson, *Australian Christmas Book* (Sydney: Lansdowne Press, 1965), 48-49.

Scrooge and the Night Before Christmas

by Nora Burdett and Karen Keller

CAST:

SCROOGE   Dressed in nightshirt and nightcap. Grumbling and acting like the absent-minded professor. He's a bit of a nervous sort.

GHOST I   Young and white-haired, dressed in a white robe.

GHOST II   Large, carrying a flashlight.

GHOST III   Stooped, wearing black.

All ghosts should be wearing very big tennis shoes to make them look strangely funny. The humor in this skit lies in your choice of cast and their ability to be animated in their portrayal of characters.

PROPS:

A bell
An old bed
Enlarged drawing of tombstone
Window

NARRATOR: Charles Dickens was a great English author who wrote *A Christmas Carol* over 100 years ago. His main character was Ebenezer Scrooge, who had plenty of money but no Christmas spirit. He hated the holiday and said it was "a poor excuse for picking a man's pockets every year. Bah, humbug!" He had a wonderful nephew and could have enjoyed Christmas with him if only he had the right Christmas spirit. Because of time, we are greatly condensing the events of that evening that changed Scrooge's life. OK—here he is now.

SCROOGE *(enters grumbling about the cold, the season, and so on; lies down and covers up to go to sleep):* Bah, Humbug!

(After a short while, the bells toll. Have someone unseen ring a bell.)

GHOST I *(SCROOGE awakens frightened):* I am the Ghost of Christmas Past—*your* past. You used to be different. You enjoyed life, but as your life began to taste success, you left everything worthwhile and noble to fulfill your greed for money. You even lost a lovely young lady because of it.

SCROOGE: Oh, no! Go away! This is too painful! *(Covers his head and tries to go back to sleep.)*

(GHOST I leaves.)

GHOST II *(shines flashlight in SCROOGE's face; he awakens again, frightened):* Look over here! Your family is able to laugh and enjoy the many pleasures of life. Look. *Look* at them. Now look at yourself; you could be enjoying yourself with them if you weren't so selfish. You are a miserable wretch indeed!

*(SCROOGE covers his head again, not wanting to see, and goes back to sleep, only to be awakened again by the next ghost, who **really** frightens him.)*

GHOST III: I am going to show you your own future.

SCROOGE: I fear you more than any of the others before you.

GHOST III: You *should* fear, for this is indeed a grim sight to behold.

(SCROOGE tries to hide his face but looks at the ghost anyway.)

GHOST III: You *must* look. You have a loyal employee, Bob Cratchit. Look at his wonderful family. *(Gestures to offstage area.)* Look closely.

SCROOGE *(looks):* They are all there . . . except . . . the little place by the fire is empty. Where's . . . Tiny Tim?

GHOST III: Gone! Yes, I said *gone*—because there was not enough money for the medical help he needed.

SCROOGE: Oh, no—this is terrible! I can't look anymore!

GHOST III: But you *must!* Now—look over at the graveyard and see that tombstone.

SCROOGE: What? It says, "Ebenezer Scrooge"! Why, that's *me* who died—and my tombstone is forgotten and unkempt. Oh, no! This is terrible! Give me another chance! I will honor Christmas in my heart and keep it all year through. I've learned my lesson. Please give me another chance!

(In the midst of all of SCROOGE's pleading, the GHOST falls quickly behind his bed. SCROOGE realizes that he has been dreaming. He hears the church bells ringing—it is Christmas Day! He gets up, opens the window, and calls down.)

SCROOGE: What day is it, my fine fellow? *(Pause)* Did you say Christmas? Wonderful! I still have time to make this Christmas wonderful for my family and to change things. I must get dressed. *(Turns to leave room and then turns back to the audience.)* By the way, Merry Christmas and God bless you!

NARRATOR: There you have it: visits from the ghosts of Christmas, and old "humbug" Scrooge changes. Let this be a lesson to you, or these ghosts may come to visit *you!*

St. Lucia's Crown

Using a Styrofoam ring or a wooden embroidery hoop, attach candle holders into the ring or hoop to hold 6" white candles. Cover the ring or hoop with greenery. Add bright ribbons to hang down the back.

Traditional Danish Hearts

Fig. 1 Cut two paper strips about 8" x 3" from different-colored paper. Fold in half lengthwise.

Fig. 2 Cut around the unfolded ends to form a rounded edge. Cut a center slit that is exactly the same length (3") as the width of the folded edge.

Figs. 3, 4, 5 Weave the paper pieces together to form a heart.

Fig. 6 Glue on a loop of yarn for hanging the heart on the tree.

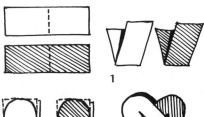

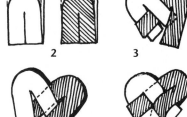

Merry Christmas in Many Languages

Type the following list, mixing the countries and their greetings. Distribute copies. Set a time limit and see who can connect the most correctly. Good for you if you can pronounce even a few of them!

ARMENIA—*Schenorhavor Dzenount*
BELGIUM (Flemish)—*Vrolijke Kerstmis*
BRAZIL (Portuguese)—*Boas Festas*
CHINA—*Kung Hsi Hsin Nien* (Or *Bing Chu Shen Tan*)
CZECHOSLOVAKIA—*Vesele Vanoce*
DENMARK—*Glaedelig Jul*
ESTONIA—*Roomsaid Joulu Puhi*
FINLAND—*Hauskaa Joulua*
FRANCE—*Joyeux Noël*
GERMANY—*Fröhliche Weihnachten*
GREECE—*Kala Christougena*
HOLLAND—*Zalig Kerstfeest*
HUNGARY—*Boldog Karacsony*
IRAQ—*Idah Saidan Wa Sanah Jadidah*
IRELAND (Gaelic)—*Nodlaig Nait Cugat*
ITALY—*Buon Natale*
JAPAN—*Meri Kurisumasu*
MEXICO—*Feliz Navidad*
NORWAY—*Gledelig Jul*
POLAND—*Wesolych Swiat*
ROMANIA—*Sarbatori Vesele*
RUSSIA—*S Roshestvóm Khristóvym*
SOUTH AFRICA (Afrikaans)—*Een Plesierige Kerfees*
SPAIN—*Felices Pascuas*
SWEDEN—*Glad Jul*
TURKEY—*Noeliniz Ve Yeni Yiliniz Kutlu Olsun*
UKRAINE—*Chrystos Rozdzajetsia Slawyte Jeho*
WALES—*Nadolig Llawen*[2]

Christmas Visitor

One of America's great poets, Edward Markham, has written a delightful poem about Conrad, a cobbler who loved his Lord. Conrad had a dream that Christ was coming to visit him at Christmas. So fully believing that, he worked hard to get his house in order for the special Guest's visit. He fixed a wonderful meal in anticipation. After he had cleaned, decorated, and cooked, he sat to wait for his honored Visitor.

He had three visitors that day, but not the one he had expected. The first was an old beggar, whom Conrad took in and warmed. He then gave him a new pair of shoes as he left. The second was a little old lady carrying a heavy load of firewood. He brought her in too, warmed her, and fed her before sending her on her way. Finally a little lost child came to his door, frightened and cold. Conrad knew he must take the child home but was fearful of missing his long-awaited Guest. Sense of duty reigned, and he took the child home.

Arriving back at his shop home, he was sure he had missed the Lord. When he asked the Lord if he had missed Him or why the Lord's

---

2. Adapted from Joan Winmill Brown, *Best of Christmas Joys* (Garden City, N.Y.: Doubleday & Co., 1983), 28-29.

feet were delaying coming, he heard a soft reply, saying that He had indeed come three times that day: in the beggar with bruised feet, in the woman he gave to eat, and in the child in a homeless street.

"And the King shall answer and say unto them, Verily I say unto you, Inasmuch as ye have done it unto one of the least of these my brethren, ye have done it unto me" (Matt. 25:40). How is it in your shop, your home, your church? Are you willing to open your doors to those who have little or nothing? Do you look for those who have needs you can meet? Jesus said that as we do it unto the least of these, we do it unto Him. Is there any room for Him in the inn of your heart? (The song "No Room," written by John W. Peterson, would be very appropriate now.)

Australian Sausage Rolls

> 4 cans crescent dinner rolls
> 2 12-ounce packages ground pork sausage (mild or hot)
> 1 medium onion, finely grated
> 1 medium carrot, finely grated
> 1 cup dry bread crumbs

Preheat oven to 350° F.

Open cans of crescent rolls and divide dough in each in half. This will give you 8 sections of dough (2 from each can). Unroll dough and press all perforations together to seal and make solid rectangles of dough.

Grate onion and carrot and mix with sausage meat. Add bread crumbs and stir until well mixed.

Divide meat mixture into 8 sections. Place ⅛ meat mixture down center of each section of dough. Fold one side of dough over meat. Fold other side of dough over and seal edges. Turn each roll over gently so that the seam side is down. Cut each roll into 12 equal portions, and place seam side down on cookie sheet. Cut small slit in top of each crust. Bake 15 minutes or until golden brown. Serve warm with ketchup.

Yield: 96 sausage rolls.

(Note: Puff pastry could be used instead of the crescent rolls and is actually more authentic, but sometimes it is more expensive and harder to find. Also, using "light" sausage means less fat.)

English Trifle

> 2 cups diced angel food, pound, or sponge cake
> ¼ cup orange juice
> 1 16-ounce can fruit cocktail, drained
> 1 6-ounce package strawberry or raspberry gelatin
> 1 4.6-ounce package vanilla pudding (may be instant)
> 1 8-ounce carton whipped dessert topping

Use a large serving bowl for making trifle. A clear bowl is recommended, since it will show the different layers.

First layer: Cake pieces, sprinkled with ¼ cup orange juice. Arrange evenly in bottom of bowl.

Second layer: Prepare gelatin according to package directions. When just thickened, add fruit cocktail. Spoon on top of first layer and refrigerate until set.

Third layer: Prepare vanilla pudding according to package directions. Mix with half the whipped dessert topping and spread on top of second layer.

Fourth layer: Spread remaining whipped topping on top of pudding. Decorate with grated chocolate, toasted nuts, kiwi slices, strawberries, or mint leaves. Chill well several hours before serving.

Bizcochitos

1 cup lard or shortening	½ cup sugar
1 egg	3 cups flour
1½ teaspoons baking powder	½ teaspoon salt
1 teaspoon anise seed	3 tablespoons orange juice
¼ cup sugar	1 tablespoon cinnamon

Cream lard and sugar. Add egg and beat until very fluffy. Sift together flour, baking powder, and salt; add to creamed mixture. Stir in juice and anise seed. Roll dough on floured board to ¼" thick and cut in squares or fancy shapes. Combine ¼ cup sugar and 1 tablespoon cinnamon, and sprinkle on top of each cookie. Bake in preheated 350° F. oven 15 to 20 minutes or until light brown. Freezes well.

Mexican Hot Chocolate

¼ cup unsweetened cocoa	¼ cup sugar
¾ teaspoon cinnamon	Dash salt
1 quart milk	¼ cup cream
¾ teaspoon vanilla	

Combine the cocoa, sugar, cinnamon, and salt, and mix well. In medium saucepan, heat 1 cup milk until bubbling. Stir in cocoa mixture; beat with wire whisk until smooth. Over low heat, bring to boil. Stir constantly. Gradually stir in remaining milk. Return to boil. Stir in cream and vanilla; heat gently. Before serving, beat with wire whisk until frothy.

Swedish Meatballs

1 onion, minced	1 teaspoon salt
3 tablespoons butter	⅛ teaspoon pepper
1 pound lean ground beef	3 tablespoons flour
½ pound each lean ground pork and veal	2 cups meat stock or consommé
1 cup dry stale bread crumbs	Pinch of grated lemon rind
1 cup milk	1 cup dairy sour cream
2 eggs, beaten	Chopped dill or parsley
Dash nutmeg	Cooked noodles

1. Saute onion in 1 tablespoon butter. Add to onion, beef, pork, veal, bread crumbs, milk, eggs, nutmeg, salt, and pepper, mixing with hands to get an even texture. Roll into small balls. Brown in 2 tablespoons butter. Remove meatballs. Add flour and stock to pan juices to make gravy. Stir until hot. Check seasoning and add lemon rind. Gravy should not be too thick at this point.

2. Return meatballs to gravy and simmer one hour over very low heat. With slotted spoon, remove meatballs to serving dish.

3. Stir sour cream into gravy and heat. Pour over meat; add dill. Serve with noodles. Makes 6 to 8 servings.

Swedish Tea Cakes

½ cup powdered sugar
1 cup margarine or butter, softened
2 teaspoons vanilla
2 cups flour
1 cup finely chopped or ground almonds or pecans
¼ teaspoon salt

Heat oven to 325° F. In large bowl, combine sugar, margarine or butter, and vanilla. Blend well. Stir in remaining ingredients until dough holds together. Shape into 1" balls. Place 1" apart on ungreased cookie sheet. Bake for 15 to 20 minutes or until set but not brown. Immediately remove from cookie sheet. Cool slightly; roll in powdered sugar. Cool completely; roll again in powdered sugar. Yields approximately 60 tea cakes (cookies).

WINTER WONDERLAND

Options

Family Party	Ladies' Party	Christmas Outreach
Christmas in July	Children's Party	

Decorations

Tables   Cover with white paper tablecloths to represent snow. Use ice-blue napkins.

Centerpieces [Yule Logs]   For each table, use a small log with three holes drilled in it, with a red candle in each hole. The center candle should be taller than the two end ones. Use evergreen branches or silk and plastic Christmas greenery and Christmas balls to decorate the log. Spray with artificial snow.

Program Covers   (See Appendix, Item 1-C.)

Name Tags   (See Appendix, Item 1-D.)

Snowflakes and Icicles   Buy or make them, and hang them all around the room for atmosphere.

Special Features

Music   Quartet or trio sing "Winter Wonderland," "White Christmas," or a Christmas medley.

Game   "Name That Christmas Tune" with Christmas carols. Have the pianist play a few notes of the carol and the guests write down the name of the song. If appropriate, award prizes for the greatest number of correct answers.

Festive Fashion Parade   (See Resources.)

Christmas Aroma   Have potpourri favors for guests and for creating a lovely, fragrant atmosphere in the party room. (See Resources.)

Cookie Decorating Demonstration   Use store-bought cookies and decorate with holly leaves and berries. Round cookies with holes in the center can be decorated as wreaths. Decorate square and rectangular ones as gifts.

Gift Box   Rather than a gift exchange, have each person bring a gift marked for a man, woman, boy, or girl to be distributed to missionaries, servicemembers, college students, orphans, nursing home residents, or the needy. If sending overseas, these should be gathered in July.

Videotape on Snow   Check your local library or Christian bookstore for *Treasures of the Snow* (adapted from a book by the same title by Patricia M. St. John), or *Hidden Treasures,* another videotape on snow.

Poems on Snow   Choose a favorite poem about snow. *Ideals* books are a good resource.

Devotional

Thoughts on Snow

1. A snowfall is a blessing. For a little while it hides the damage generally seen in our man-scarred world.
2. The proportion of water that makes snowflakes is two parts hydrogen to one part oxygen. Its nuclear structure produces a triangular shape, reminding us of the Trinity.
3. While all snowflakes are made of the same substance, their atoms and molecules are arranged differently as they fall through the atmosphere. Each one is unique.
4. Isa. 1:18.
5. Job 38:22.

Food

Potluck dinner featuring favorite Christmas recipes.

RESOURCES

Festive Fashion Parade

by Nora Burdett and Karen Keller

Slip-over cardigan (sweater) A nylon slip worn over a sweater.

Fourteen-carrot necklace A very basic dark dress and a necklace of 14 carrots strung on fine rope.

Tent dress You guessed it, but find the smallest tent you can!

Tissue dress Facial tissues pinned or taped by one corner all over a basic dark dress so that they give the garment a ragged look. Start at the hem of the dress and work your way up.

Afternoon tea dress A simple dress with tea bags attached like fringe around the yoke, sleeves, hem, halfway up the skirt, or a combination of these. (Designed by your favorite brand of tea.)

Print dress A lovely dress fashioned from the latest newspaper. (It is really "a flashy bit of news.")

Checked dress Several canceled checks taped or pinned all over a dress.

Nylon dress Old panty hose (clean ones, of course) attached all over a basic dress.

Plunging neckline A new toilet plunger worn around the neck, tied on with ribbon or string. A toilet paper bow in the hair finishes off the ensemble. Model could carry a toilet paper roll "handbag" just for fun.

Hand-painted shirt One of hubby's old shirts he uses for painting, worn with a plain skirt. Add more detail with various sizes and colors of handprints painted all over the shirt. (Designed by your favorite paint brand.)

End by saying, "This concludes our Festive Fashion Parade, brought to you by Nickel's" (instead of Penney's).

Christmas Aroma

Combine the following ingredients in a teakettle or saucepan, bring to a boil, and simmer. Creates a nice, fragrant atmosphere.

3 (4") cinnamon sticks
¼ cup whole cloves
3 bay leaves
1 or 2 lemons, halved
1 quart water

Make the mix of dry ingredients ahead of time, wrapped nicely in nylon net or tulle. Give to each person as he or she leaves. Be sure to include instructions for use.

A Victorian Christmas

Options

Christmas in July   Women's Outreach

Decorations

Tables   Cover with soft pink tablecloths.

Centerpieces   Oblong evergreen arrangement. Stick freshly cut evergreen into potatoes on all sides to make a nice oblong shape. Decorate with little fans, loops of ribbon, and puffs of tulle all fastened on wires or toothpicks. Add these decoratively to the greenery on the potato. Use bright pink, soft pink, and ivory. Candles could be added, or use oil lamps.

Program Cover   (See Appendix, Item 1-E.)

Name Tags   (See Appendix, Item 1-F.)

Christmas Wreaths   These wreaths are inexpensive, made from unbleached muslin, decorated with bright pink and silver. They can be sold at the end of the program to recoup the cost of making. (See Resources.)

Victorian Christmas Angel   Hang just inside the door to welcome the guests. (See Appendix, Item 1-G.)

Pink Fans   (See Resources.)

Christmas Tree   Decorate tree with a variety of Victorian ornaments and lots of tiny white lights.

Accents   Inside the door, place on an easel a large piece of pink cardboard with "Welcome to a Victorian Christmas," followed by the dinner (or light) menu. Quilts, oil lamps, old dolls, teddy bears, etc., will achieve a soft Victorian look.

Special Features

Quartet or Trio   Present several arrangements of Christmas songs. The audience could be invited to participate. Sleigh bells add a special Christmas touch. If costumes are available, have the group dress Victorian.

Games   (See Resources.)

Demonstrations

- Make fudge, divinity, or molded chocolates.
- Show various ways of wrapping and decorating Christmas gifts.
- Victorian hanky dolls. These were made for little girls to play with in Victorian times. Today they make lovely tree decorations. (See Resources.)
- Quick apron from a dishtowel. (See Resources.)

Devotional

A Victorious Christmas   (See Resources.)

Food

Dinner Menu
    Baked ham
    Scalloped potatoes
    Broccoli
    Old-fashioned bread pudding
    Tea and coffee

Light Menu
    Dainty cakes and sandwiches

RESOURCES

Christmas Wreaths

Materials needed for one wreath:

- unbleached muslin or calico strips, 20" x 88" (no seams if possible)
- cardboard
- trimmings for wreath (ribbon, decorations, etc.)

How to make wreath:

Fig. 1   Fold, sew, and turn the strip of muslin, making very small seams. Press flat.

Fig. 2   Sew a straight line 1½" from folded edge. This makes the ruffle on the inside of the wreath. Sew 3½" up from last seam to form the casing for cardboard.

Fig. 3   Cut a 13" circle out of good-quality cardboard. Measure in 3" and mark. Then cut out center of wreath. Along the grain of cardboard, make a slit so that the fabric can be gathered onto it by gently pushing the fabric onto the cardboard ring. Make sure that the slit in the cardboard ring is at the bottom of wreath.

Fig. 4   When all the fabric is gathered on the cardboard, reinforce and close slits in the ring with tape. Pull fabric together and handstitch. Adjust ruffles evenly and decorate both sides if it is going to hang from the ceiling, one side if you are going to use it against the wall.

Pink Fans

Materials needed:

- printed wallpaper scraps or wrapping paper
- lace
- ribbon
- wire

Fig. 1   a. The paper you use for making fans should be 2½ to 3 times as long as it is wide. This makes a nice full fan when finished. The longer the paper, the fuller the fan.

          b. Before folding, sew with a long stitch, or glue, straight lace along the full length of one side.

Fig. 2   Fold back and forth in accordion style, making sure to keep folds straight and even.

Fig. 3   Secure gathered end of fan with fine wire. Spread the lace

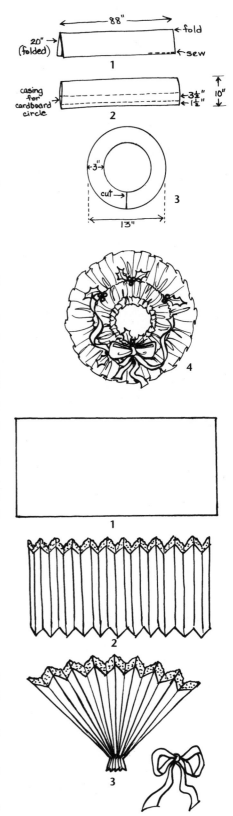

end out gently, making a lovely fan. Add ribbon to base or handle of fan.

Games (Choose one)

1. Copy a Victorian picture (a very complex, busy one from a book or magazine). Give a copy to each guest for 30 seconds. Have each guest write down in 60 seconds as many things as he or she can remember.

2. Spices were of great value in Victorian times. In plastic bags, put small amounts of various spices (one per bag). Seal each bag tightly and number it. Pass numbered bags around and ask each person to write down the name of each spice without smelling it.

3. Plum pudding was a favorite Victorian dessert. Four surprises were commonly found inside. See if the guests can figure out the significance of each:

A thimble—An old maid

A sixpence—Riches will come

A button—A bachelor

A ring—First one to marry

Victorian Hanky Doll

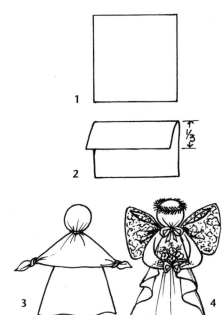

Materials needed:
- Handkerchief
- Styrofoam ball or stuffing for head
- Lace for bow wings
- Ribbon for neck and bouquet
- Gold chenille wire for halo
- Flowers for bouquet
- Hot glue gun and clear glue

Fig. 1   Start with a square handkerchief.

Fig. 2   Fold ⅓ of handkerchief down over remaining handkerchief.

Fig. 3   Put Styrofoam ball or stuffing in center of folded area. Gather handkerchief around head and tie with string to form the head of the angel. Tie knots in the short folded-over corners to make hands.

Fig. 4   Bring hands around to the front side of doll and secure hands as they hold a bouquet of flowers. Attach bow to bouquet of flowers and neck of angel. Arrange the skirt attractively behind the arms. Glue gold metallic chenille wire around head for halo. Glue bow to back of angel just below head for wings. Attach a loop of gold cord with the bow for hanging on the tree.

Quick Apron from a Dish Towel

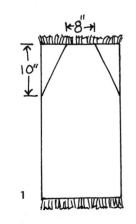

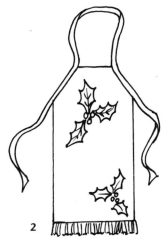

Materials needed:
- Linen or terry dish towel
- 2½ yards double-folded bias tape

Fig. 1   If towel is fringed, fold fringe down and stitch for the top of apron. Leave fringe at bottom of apron. Cut away corners as shown in diagram.

Fig. 2   Keep bias tape in one piece. Stitch 24" together for first tie; bind the right-hand cut edge of apron; stitch next 18" of tape together for neck; bind left-hand cut edge of apron; stitch last 24" of tape for second tie.

A Victorious Christmas

I remember a day one winter that stands out like a boulder in my life. The weather was unusually cold; our salary had not been regularly paid, and it did not meet our needs when it was. What a contrast to a more comfortable and elegant life back East in my Victorian home!

My husband, James, was away much of the time, traveling from one district to another. Our boys were well, but my little Ruth was ailing, and at best none of us was decently clothed. I patched and repatched, with spirits sinking to their lowest ebb. The water was frozen in the well, and the wind blew through the cracks in the floor.

The people in the village were kind and generous, but the settlement was new, and each family was struggling for itself. Little by little, at the time I needed it most, my faith began to waver.

Early in life I was taught to take God at His Word, and I thought my lesson was well learned. I had lived upon the promises in dark times until I knew, as David did, who my Fortress and Deliverer was. Now a daily prayer for forgiveness was all I could offer.

My husband's overcoat was hardly thick enough for winter, and he was often obliged to ride miles to attend a meeting or funeral. Many times our breakfast was Indian cake and a cup of tea without sugar.

Christmas was coming; the children always expected their presents. The ice was thick and smooth, and the boys were each craving a pair of skates. Ruth, in some unaccountable way, had taken a fancy that the dolls I had made were no longer suitable; she wanted a nice large one and insisted on praying for it.

I knew it was impossible, but, oh, how I wanted to give each child his present. It seemed as if God had deserted us. But I did not tell my husband all this. He worked so earnestly and heartily I supposed him to be as hopeful as ever. I kept the sitting room cheerful with an open fire and tried to serve our scanty meals as invitingly as I could.

The morning before Christmas, James was called to see a sick man. I packed a piece of bread for his lunch—it was the best I could do—wrapped my plaid shawl around his neck, and then tried to whisper a promise as I often had, but the words died away upon my lips. I let him go without it.

That was a dark, hopeless day. I coaxed the children to bed early, for I could not bear their talk. I paused to listen to Ruth's prayer. She asked the last time most explicitly for her doll and for skates for her brothers. Her bright face looked so lovely when she whispered to me, "You know, I think they will be here early tomorrow morning, Mama." With that, I wished I could move heaven and earth to save her from disappointment. Then I sat down alone and gave way to the most bitter tears.

Before long James returned chilled and exhausted. He drew off his boots. The thin stockings slipped off with them, and his feet were red with cold. "I wouldn't treat a dog that way, let alone a faithful servant," I said. Then as I glanced up and saw the hard lines in his face and the look of despair, it flashed across my soul that James had let go too.

I brought him a cup of tea, feeling sick and dizzy at the very thought. He took my hand, and we sat for an hour without a word. I wanted to die and meet God and tell Him His promises weren't true; my soul was so full of rebellious despair.

There came a sound of bells, a quick step, and a loud knock at the door. James sprang up to open it. There stood Brother White. He said, "A box came by express just before dark. I brought it around as soon as I could get away. Reckoned it might be for Christmas. I thought you should have it tonight. Here is a turkey my wife asked me to fetch, along with these other things I believe belong to you." There was a basket of potatoes and a bag of flour. Talking all the time, he hurried in with the box, and then with a hearty good-night he rode away.

Still without speaking, James found a chisel and opened the box. He drew out first a thick red blanket, and we saw that beneath it the box was full of clothing. It seemed at that moment as if Christ fastened upon me a look of reproach.

James sat down and covered his face with his hands. "I can't touch them," he explained. "I haven't been true, just when God was trying to see if I could hold out. Do you think I could not see how you were suffering? And I had no words of comfort to offer. I know now how to preach the awfulness of turning away from God."

"James," I said, clinging to him, "don't take it to heart like this. I am to blame. I ought to have helped you. We will ask Him together to forgive us."

"Wait a moment, dear; I cannot talk now." Then he went into another room, and I knelt down and my heart broke. In an instant all the darkness, all the stubbornness rolled away! Jesus came again and stood before me, with the loving word "Daughter!" Sweet promises of tenderness and joy flooded my soul. I was so lost in praise and thanksgiving that I forgot everything else. I do not know how long it was before James came back, but I knew he, too, had found peace.

"Now, my dear wife," he said, "let us thank God together," and he then poured out scriptural words of praise, for nothing else could express our thanksgiving.

It was eleven o'clock; the fire was low, and there was the great box with nothing touched but the warm blanket we needed. We piled on some fresh logs, lit two candles, and began to examine our treasures.

We drew out an overcoat. I made James try it on—just the right size—and I danced around him, for all my lightheartedness had returned. Then there was a cloak, and he insisted on seeing me in it. My spirits always infected him, and we both laughed like foolish children.

There was a warm suit of clothes also, and three pairs of woolen stockings. There was a dress for me and yards of flannel, a pair of arctic overshoes for each of us, and in mine a slip of paper. I have it now and mean to hand it down to my children. It was Moses' blessing to Asher: "Thy shoes shall be iron and brass; and as thy days, so shall thy strength be [Deut. 33:25]." In the gloves evidently for James, the same dear hand had written: "I the Lord thy God will hold thy right hand, saying unto thee, Fear not; I will help thee" [Isa. 41:13].

It was a wonderful box packed with thoughtful care. There was a suit of clothes for each of the boys and a little red gown for Ruth. There were mittens, scarves, and hoods, and down in the center, a box. We opened it, and there was a great wax doll! I burst into tears again, and James wept with me for joy. It was too much! And then we both wept again, for close behind it came two pairs of skates. There were books for us to read—some of them I had wished to see—stories for the children to read, aprons and underclothing, knots of ribbon, a lovely photograph, needles, buttons and thread, actually a muff, and an envelope containing a $10.00 gold piece.

At last we cried over everything we took up. It was past midnight, and we were faint and exhausted even with happiness. I made a cup of tea, cut a fresh loaf of bread, and James boiled some eggs. We drew up the table before the fire. How we enjoyed our supper! And then we sat talking over our life and how sure a help God had always proved.

You should have seen the children on Christmas morning. The boys raised a shout at the sight of their skates. Ruth caught up her doll and hugged it tightly without a word; then she went to her room and knelt by her bed.

When she came back she whispered to me, "I knew it would be here, Mama, but I wanted to thank God just the same, you know."

"Look here, wife. See the difference!" We went to the window, and there were the boys out of the house already and skating on the crust with all their might.

My husband and I both tried to return thanks to the church in the East that sent us the box and have tried to return thanks unto God every day since.

Hard times have come again and again, but we have trusted in Him—dreading nothing so much as our doubt of His protecting care. "But they that seek the Lord shall not want any good thing" [Ps. 34:10].[1]

---

1. Adapted from "Christmas Time on the Frontier," *Sword of the Lord,* December 7, 1973, 1, 6. This story, told by an anonymous pastor's wife, has been reprinted numerous times by *Sword of the Lord,* which has not been able to trace the name of the author.

BEARY MERRY CHRISTMAS

Options

Christmas in July   Outreach
Ladies' Party   Family Party   Children's Party

Decorations

Serving Table   Use a red tablecloth.

Group Tables   Cover with white paper that has been stamped with pictures of little teddy bears. Each table has a hostess, who hands out materials and handles other details.

Centerpieces   Folded brown paper bears among evergreen, decorations, and/or candles. (See Resources.)

Program Covers   (See Appendix, Item 1-H.)

Name Tags   Use the basic bear pattern (Appendix, Item 1-I), or place a bear stamp or stickers on 2½" x 4" cards.

Musical Bears Mural   (See Resources.)

Teddy Bears   Display beloved family teddy bears brought by the guests. Put a string around the necks of the bears so that they can be fastened to the wall. Then invite guests to judge and vote for

1. the oldest teddy
2. the most-loved teddy
3. the most unusual teddy

Christmas Tree   Decorate the Christmas tree with red-and-white bear garland. (See Resources.) Make other bears using basic bear pattern in several sizes on red and white construction paper. Use a punch to make a hole between the ears on the head, and run ribbon or gold cord through to hang on the tree. Red-and-white paper chain made in one of the games can be added to the tree. Tiny blinking lights and icicles make a beary beautiful tree. Top the tree with an angel bear, using the basic bear pattern. Add gold chenille wire for halo and large bow on the back for wings.

Special Features

The Bear and/or Bear Helper   Either find a person to wear a bear costume or choose someone to put on the "Official Bear Helper" badge (see Appendix, Item 1-J) and bear ears on a headband. (See Resources.)

Gift Certificates   Copy on bright red paper, one for each individual. (See Appendix, Item 1-K.)

Christmas Bears for Nursing Home   (See Resources.)

Games

Tear a teddy bear (See Resources.)

Paper chain (See Resources.)

Surprise box (See Resources.)

Skit—"What If He Had Not Come?"   (See Resources.)

Bear Bags   A small paper bag stamped with pictures of bears is given to each guest. The bag contains:

    1. Bear letter (See Appendix, Item 1-L.)
    2. Gummy bear candy
    3. Ginger bear cookie recipe and sample cookies (See Resources.)
    4. Herbal tea bear (See Resources.)

Personal Storytelling   Guests tell about their first Christmas away from home. Find the best Christmas story at each table. Short stories may be shared during refreshments or as a game or contest.

The Three Bear Facts

This program contains all the special features listed above and is an integral part of this entire evening. (See Resources.)

    The first bear fact—Crafts

    The second bear fact—Games and Refreshments

    The third bear fact—Devotional

Devotional

The third "bear fact" includes the devotional for the evening.

Food

Sausage cheese balls (See Resources.)

Caramel corn

Hot apple cider

Suggested Order of Events

1. Welcome/Skit.
2. First bear fact.
3. Make Christmas bears for nursing homes.
4. Fill out gift certificates.
5. Second bear fact.
6. Tear a teddy.
7. Make a paper chain.
8. Surprise box creation.
9. Judging teddys.
10. Refreshments and personal storytelling.
11. Third bear fact.
12. Devotional—"What If He Had Not Come?"
13. Carol singing.
14. Give out bear bags.

RESOURCES

Welcome or Prelude to the Evening

CAST—Bear or "Official Bear Helper" and Mother

SETTING—A weary mother falls asleep while wrapping last-minute gifts. The Christmas Bear encourages her.

MOTHER *(depressed):* Christmas spirit? If there *is* such a thing, I've lost it. I'm so tired, I've spent too much money, and half of the gifts probably won't be appreciated or will be broken before Christmas Day is over. And now I'm worried about those I have forgotten. Every year I think it will be different, but every year I'm late getting the shopping done, spend too much money, and make wrong choices for gifts. I become grouchy and am too tired to enjoy Christmas the way I should. Maybe if I just lay my head down here for a minute I'll feel . . . *(falls asleep).*

BEAR or HELPER *(comes in and moves over beside the mother as she awakes):* Hello! I am here to teach you the "bear facts" of Christmas. We bears have been around for a long time and have seen many a Christmas. So you can count on me to give you the "three bear facts." *(Turns toward audience.)* It is wonderful to have you at our "Beary Merry Christmas" party. Is everyone settled? Now, if our hostess will come, we will get on with the "bear facts" of Christmas.

(At this point the MOTHER leaves, and the table and packages are removed.)

The Three Bear Facts

Each is presented by the Bear or Bear Helper.

I. *The first bear fact is that Christmas is for giving.* (Crafts)
God gave His only begotten Son to die on the Cross for us. The wise men gave gifts to the Christ child. The heartbeat of Christmas is giving. You may have spent hundreds of dollars on expensive gifts for people who already have everything. How much better to give something of *yourself!* Here's how you can put this first "bear fact" into practice.
   A. Make "Beary Merry Christmas" bears to put on the meal trays of nursing home residents. That would be a "beary" special treat on Christmas Day. (See Appendix, Item 1-I.)
   B. Give a certificate filled in with a special gift of love and service.
      1. Go walking with someone who needs to walk for his or her health.
      2. Give a casserole for a busy day.
      3. Offer to baby-sit.
      4. Give an IOU for a homegrown garden vegetable.

II. *The second bear fact is that Christmas should be a time of homespun fun.* (Games and Refreshments)
This isn't expensive. It just takes imagination, time spent together, and a little planning.
   A. *Tear a teddy bear*   Give each of your guests a sheet of white paper, and while holding it behind their backs they each try to tear out a teddy bear (one-minute time limit).
   B. *Paper chain*   Distribute precut paper strips and glue sticks; see which table or group can make the longest chain in five minutes. Use to decorate the tree.
   C. *Surprise box*   Give each table a box containing a variety of things typically used to make something related to Christmas. Offer a prize to the group that is most creative in using the most arti-

cles in a 12-minute time limit. Supplies in the box could include yarn, a paper plate, tape, glue, felt, pins, red and green paper, ribbon, craft sticks, large sheet of white paper, cotton balls, black felt pen, scissors, paper cup, buttons, etc.

D. *Teddy bear judging contest*   Each person votes for his or her choice of oldest, most-loved, or most unusual bear. Tally the results, and at the end of the evening give a prize for each category.

III. *The third bear fact is that Christ is the real reason for the Christmas season.* (Devotional)

Sometimes we get caught up in the hustle and bustle and forget that Christmas is a time to remember the birth of our Savior. He is the real reason we have Christmas. Shut your eyes for a moment, and go with me to a little homestead house on the southwestern prairie and see what we can learn.

What If He Had Not Come?

by Nora Burdett and Karen Keller

CHARACTERS: MOTHER
              Two or more children

SETTING: Rocking chair
              Small table with Bible on it
              Oil lamp and/or hatstand

The lights are dimmed, and the characters are spotlighted. A little family has just received word that the father isn't going to make it home for Christmas. The children are upset and wonder how they can possibly have Christmas without Daddy and especially without the presents they are sure he would have brought. After a time of feeling sorry for themselves, Mother speaks to them:

MOTHER: Now children, I think we are looking at this the wrong way. We have been so worried about whether Daddy will come, or whether Grandma and Grandpa will come, or whether we will have any presents. But think for a moment. What if Jesus had not come? Why, today wouldn't be any different from yesterday or tomorrow.

There would be no need for the Christmas tree or decorations if He had not come. If you were sick or troubled, there would be no words of encouragement and no hope, because Jesus would not have risen from the dead. There would be no church to go to on Sunday if Jesus had not come. There would be no Christmas carols to sing. All this we would miss if He had not come.

You know, one day you will be grown, and perhaps you will be living a long way from Mother and Daddy, but you can still have Christmas in your hearts. Christmas has nothing to do with the nearness of friends and relatives, or with Christmas presents, special foods, Christmas carols, snow, or anything else. We can enjoy the Christmas spirit without any of these things, because we simply thank God for His "unspeakable gift"—Jesus.

"Do you remember a Bible verse that tells about the special Gift God gave us? Yes, it is John 3:16. *(Have one of the children quote it.)* Do you remember another verse that reminds us why He came?

Yes, it is Isa. 53:6. *(Have another child quote it.)* Now, let me read the Christmas story to you. *(Read Luke 2:1-20.)*

We can be glad and rejoice tonight, because "He *has* come." We aren't alone, and we have the best present ever. What joy Jesus has brought to our home! Here—let's light a little candle and sing "Joy to the World," because the Lord has come. I'm sure the whole world will sing it with us.

Sing a few carols as the hostesses light the candles at each table. Dim the lights (if they weren't already dimmed for the skit). As the guests depart, they are each given a "bear bag" to help them have a "Beary Merry Christmas."

Musical Bears Mural

Copy onto brown wrapping paper. Outline with wide black marking pen. Bows can be made from paper or ribbon and attached to each bear. (See Appendix, Items 1-M (a-e). Note: There are five individual bear drawings for this Appendix reference.)

Bear Ears for Official Bear Helper

Materials needed:
- clear tape
- hot glue
- one sheet brown construction paper
- one inexpensive headband

(See Appendix, Item 1-N.)

Fig. 1   For ears, cut two 4½" (diameter) circles from brown construction paper.

Fig. 2   Make a dart 3" long and ½" wide at bottom of each ear.

Fig. 3   Fold over and glue or tape to give ears a slight cupped effect.

Fig. 4   Fold ½" of circle back on bottom of each ear. Attach folded-back part of ear onto headband with glue. If ears tend to droop, use cellophane tape to hold backs of ears to headband so that they stand up.

Basic Bear Pattern

(See Appendix, Item 1-I.)

Centerpieces   Enlarge pattern on brown construction paper so that you have three different sizes of bears. Cut and fold. Add bright red or green bows at neck. Arrange with greenery, Christmas ornaments, and candles on tables.

Christmas Bears for Nursing Home   Copy onto brown construction paper. Cut out and fold on dotted lines. Tape a wrapped mint candy on the tummy or on one foot of the bear. Tape or glue the "Beary Merry Christmas" greeting to the edges of each paw. Include a large-print Christmas tract and red bow at neck if desired.

Bear Garland

(See Appendix, Item 1-O.)

Fold long strips of lightweight paper the width of your pattern. Make sure the hands and feet are on the fold so that bears will be connected at these points. Cut out and unfold garland. Eyes and nose may be made with paper punch. Use garland to decorate Christmas tree.

Ginger Bear and Herbal Tea Bear

See Appendix, Item 1-P, for patterns for the bears that go inside the bear bags. Copy these onto paper and attach a small pouch of ginger to the ginger bear (write the recipe on one side) and a herbal tea bag to the herbal tea bear, onto which you write,

Bearly making it?
Take a break!
Put your feet up for 10 minutes
   and have a cup of delicious,
      different herbal tea.
Try to figure out what kind it is.
Enjoy!

Ginger Bear Cookies

Pour ¼ cup boiling water over ½ cup butter and blend. Add ½ cup brown sugar and ½ cup dark molasses and mix. Sift together 3 cups flour, 1 teaspoon baking soda, 1 teaspoon salt, 1½ teaspoon ginger, ½ teaspoon nutmeg, ⅛ teaspoon cloves. Add to butter mix and blend. Chill and roll on floured cloth to ¼" thickness. Cut with bear-shaped cutter and bake on greased pan at 375° F. for 10 minutes.

Sausage Cheese Balls

1½ pounds hot sausage
3 cups baking mix
1 pound grated cheddar cheese

Mix all ingredients well, form into small balls, and bake at 350° F. for 15 minutes. Serve immediately. (Can be frozen and baked later.)

GIFTS THAT
KEEP ON GIVING

Options

Adult/Family Program   Teen Program   Women's Ministries Program

Decorations

Tables   Use pink tablecloths.

Centerpieces   Wrap little boxes or scrap wood blocks, all different sizes and shapes, with pink and silver gift wrap. Arrange with holly, evergreen, and candles.

Program Covers   (See Appendix, Item 1-Q.)

Name Tags   (See Appendix, Item 1-R.)

Special Features

Gift-Wrapped Choir   Gift-wrap a large box for each singer. Cut holes for the head, arms, and waist so that the box can easily be slipped over the head. Be sure each singer is dressed in a solid color.

Gift Exchange   "White elephants." Bring something from home that you no longer have use for.

Old-fashioned Box Supper   Have guests bring food neatly wrapped and sell it to the highest bidder. (Suggestions: cookies, brownies, homemade bread, jam, ice cream toppings, relish, homemade fudge) All proceeds go to a special project.

Special Gift Favor   Wrap small boxes and attach a poem to each. Give one to each guest. (See Resources.)

Puppet Play   "God's Great Gift from Above." (See Resources.)

Devotional

Gifts the Wise Men Gave   Matt. 2:11 (See Resources.)

Food

Fondue. For a different menu, collect as many fondue pots as you can and serve a choice of fondues with a variety of food items for dipping.

RESOURCES

Special Gift Favor Poem

(Author unknown)

This is a very special gift
    That you can never see.
The reason it's so special is
    It's just for you from me.
Whenever you are lonely
    Or even feeling blue,
You only have to hold this gift
    And know I think of you.
You never can unwrap it;
    Please leave the ribbon tied.
Just hold the box close to your heart—
    It's filled with love inside.

God's Great Gift from Above

by Nora Burdett and Karen Keller

CAST—All characters except TEACHER are puppets: SUZIE (girl puppet), MR. OWL, FROG, MONKEY, and SQUIRREL.

SETTING—On one side of the puppet stage, set up an easel with a flannel board. Display a Nativity scene in flannel or felt. Cover the front of the flannel scene with bright wrapping paper and a big bow. Refer to it as "the gift."

SUZIE *(enters, looking at the beautiful "gift" at one side of the puppet stage):* I wonder what's in the lovely package. I *do* love Christmastime, because it means presents for everyone. Oh, who could this one be for?

MR. OWL *(enters):* Hello, Suzie! How are you today?

SUZIE: Oh, I'm just fine, Mr. Owl. I'm so excited because it's nearly Christmas. But I'm just wondering what's in that big box. Who is it for?

MR. OWL: That present, Suzie, is for everyone in the whole world! And it's from God. It's His great gift from above. Do you know what it is, Suzie?

SUZIE: No, Mr. Owl, I don't.

MR. OWL: Well, just think about it, and I'll be back later to see if you've been able to guess what it is.

(MR. OWL leaves, FROG enters, singing his frog song to the tune of "The Old Gray Mare, She Ain't What She Used to Be.")

FROG *(singing):* "Oh, you've heard frogs go fer-odi-odeo fer-odi-odeo, fer-odi-odeo;
Oh, you've heard frogs go fer-odi-odeo.
But you've never heard a frog go gink, gank, gook."

Ribbit, ribbit, ribbit. Hello, Suzie-Q. How are you?

SUZIE: Pretty good, Frog. But I can't decide what's in that big box. Mr. Owl said it was God's great gift from above. Do you know what that could be?

FROG: Let me see—God's great gift from above. Why, yes, Suzie. I'm sure I can tell you what it is. You see, I'm very fond of something that comes from above, and that's *flies*. You see, they're my very special food, which God has made for me. Yes, I'm sure that's what's in that box.

SUZIE: Dear me, I don't know about that, Frog, because Mr. Owl said it was God's gift to everyone in the whole world, and most of us don't like flies quite as much as *you* do. No, I just don't think that package is full of flies.

FROG: Well, Suzie, I must go now, and I hope you find out just what's in that box. I must go and find some nice, juicy flies, for I'm hungry again. Good-bye now.

SUZIE: Good-bye, Frog. *(FROG leaves and MONKEY enters.)*

MONKEY: Hi, Suzie. My—you look like you're thinking about something very serious. Can I help you?

SUZIE: As a matter of fact, you can, Monkey. You see, I'm wondering what's in that beautiful box. Mr. Owl told me it was a gift for the whole world and it's from God—it's His great gift from above. What do you think it is, Monkey?

MONKEY: Oh, that's easy, Suzie, for God gave me something very wonderful from above, and all monkeys just love it—the *banana*. I'll bet that box is just full of bananas. Let me see. *(Moves over as though he is going to try to open the package.)*

SUZIE: No. Wait. Don't open it. I just don't think it could be a package of bananas. Mr. Owl said it was something for everyone, and not everyone would take too kindly to a bunch of bananas. I'll just have to keep thinking and trying to find out what God's great gift from above is. Good-bye, Monkey. *(MONKEY leaves and SQUIRREL enters.)*

SQUIRREL: Hi, Suzie, and how are you?

SUZIE: Oh, I just don't know, Squirrel, because I have a problem.

SQUIRREL: And what *is* your problem? Can I help?

SUZIE: Perhaps you can if you can tell me what's in that big box over there. Mr. Owl said it was God's great gift from above for all the world. Mr. Frog said he thought it was flies, because they come from above and give him food to eat. Mr. Monkey insisted that it was bananas, for they too come from above and are the very things he loves to eat. I'm sure they are wrong, but you, Squirrel, look like such a smart fellow. Could you tell me what God's great gift from above is?

SQUIRREL: Oh, I have it, all right. Of course, anyone knows it's *nuts*. They are the best food. They're so good that I don't need anything else as long as I live. Yes, it certainly must be nuts.

SUZIE: Oh, no, no, no! You all have your minds on food! I just think it's something so much more wonderful than food. But dear me, I just don't know what it could be. I must think, think, think. Good-bye, Squirrel. Go and enjoy some more nuts. *(Exit SQUIRREL and enter MR. OWL.)*

SUZIE: Well, I see Mr. Owl coming, so perhaps we can find out for sure what it really is.

MR. OWL: Hello again, Suzie. Tell me—have you guessed what God's great gift from above is?

SUZIE: No, Mr. Owl. But I asked Frog, and he said it was flies. Monkey said he thought it was bananas. Squirrel said he thought it was nuts. But no, I just don't know what it is yet. Will you please tell me what it is?

MR. OWL: Yes, Suzie, I have asked Mrs. _____ to come out here and show you what's in that box. She will tell you all about God's great gift from above. Perhaps while we are waiting, we can sing "Away in a Manger." *(All puppets come up, and they and the guests sing the song. As the TEACHER unwraps the "present," she begins to tell of the greatest gift God ever gave—the Lord Jesus Christ. The Christmas story unfolds, and the plan of salvation is made clear. The puppet play is basically an introduction to the Christmas story as told by the teacher.)*

TEACHER *(expound on the following thoughts, and allow for audience participation in answering questions. If your program includes families with young children, gear this puppet play and lesson to them, and everyone will get the message and enjoy the participation of the children. Begin by having someone read aloud to the audience Luke 1:26-38; 2:1-14.)*

  What is a gift? This part of the Bible tells us that Mary was going to get something very special. She and Joseph would be the first humans to see God's great gift from above. What was the gift? Yes—a baby boy. What was His name? Yes—Jesus. But did you know that this Baby wasn't just for Mary and Joseph, but for the whole world? Who can quote John 3:16? *(Have someone quote it.)* Whose son was Jesus really? Yes, God's. Jesus truly is God's great Gift from above.

  Why did God give us such a special gift as His only Son? He must love us very much. We should be really thankful (2 Cor. 9:15). But God didn't just give us His Son because He wanted to give us a gift. He knew that our sin would keep us out of heaven unless someone paid the price for it (Rom. 3:23 and 6:23). Since none of us are good enough to get to heaven by ourselves, we need someone to pay the price for us. Jesus is God's great Gift from above, the only one who can take away the sin of the world. His cousin, John the Baptist, called Jesus "the Lamb of God, which taketh away the sin of the world" (John 1:29). *(Depending on the age-group of the audience, you might want to talk about the Old Testament sacrifices that had been the means of covering sin before Jesus' blood covered sin for all time.)*

  How do we get this gift? The Bible says that God gave the

world His very own Son. What do we call something someone gives us? Yes—a gift. Do we have to pay for a gift? No. How do we get it? We just accept it or receive it. At Christmas we are reminded that God has given us a very special, perfect gift, but we must receive it if it is to become ours (John 1:12).

Gifts the Wise Men Gave
Matt. 2:11

Gold is the gift of kings and is representative of our material wealth and the splendor of royalty. Prov. 25:11—"A word fitly spoken is like apples of gold in pictures of silver." Words are powerful. They can build self-esteem and communicate or do just the opposite (see poem titled "Word Power"). Scripture references: John 1:1-14; Prov. 27:5; 15:1.

Frankincense   A resin used in incense making—a picture to us of prayer. One of the greatest gifts we can give our family, friends, or pastor is to pray for them. Scripture references: Luke 1:10; Rev. 5:8.

Myrrh   An aromatic gum resin used in embalming. Jesus laid down His life for our sin. Share the good news of the gospel.

Gift Box Demonstration

Wrap two small, empty boxes to represent gold and frankincense and secure them to a board. They remain unchanged throughout the lesson. To represent myrrh:

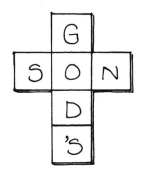

The box is cut out of light cardboard, creased on the lines so that it will fold easily.

Run a sharp instrument along a ruler's edge laid on the lines that are to be folded. Cover with red paper and use black ribbon.

Tack back side 3 to your board, and then tie box up. Untie and open so that the words "God's" and "Son" can be seen while talking about sharing the gospel.

Word Power

(Author unknown)

A gracious word may smooth the way;
A joyous word may light the day;
A timely word may lessen stress;
A loving word may heal and bless.
A careless word may kindle strife;
A cruel word may wreck a life;
A bitter word may hate instill;
A brutal word may smite and kill.

Welsh Rarebit Fondue

3 cups grated cheddar cheese
3 cups grated American cheese
2 tablespoons flour

1 can low-calorie ginger ale
1 tablespoon Worcestershire sauce
½ teaspoon dry mustard
1 tablespoon snipped chives

Toss together cheeses with flour and set aside. Pour ginger ale into fondue pan. Blend in Worcestershire sauce and dry mustard. Turn temperature to 250° F. and heat liquid just to boiling point. Lower temperature to 220° F. Add cheese mixture, about ½ cup at a time, stirring constantly. When all of cheese is blended, stir in chives. Lower temperature to 180° F.

For dipping: Sourdough bread or French bread cut into ¾" cubes, small shrimp, small chunks of ham, tiny meatballs, cherry tomatoes.

Raspberry Fondue

2 1-pound packages frozen raspberries, thawed
¼ cup granulated sugar
¼ cup cornstarch
¼ cup orange juice
1 tablespoon lemon juice

Puree raspberries, using blender or sieve. Pour pureed raspberries into cold fondue pan; blend with sugar and cornstarch. Turn temperature to 250° F. and stir raspberry mixture continually until thickened and clear. Stir in orange juice and lemon juice. Lower temperature to warm, and serve.

For dipping: Cubes of angel food, pound, or sponge cake; bananas (sliced in chunks and dipped in lemon juice); whole fresh strawberries or other fresh fruit; marshmallows.

Chocolate Fondue

¼ cup butter or margarine
1 cup evaporated milk
1 cup light corn syrup
1 12-ounce package chocolate chips
½ cup finely chopped nuts
⅓ teaspoon peppermint or almond extract (optional)

Set temperature at 220° F. and melt butter or margarine. Stir in evaporated milk and light corn syrup. Add chocolate chips, nuts, and extract if desired. Stir until chips are melted and thoroughly blended. Adjust temperature to 200° F. for serving.

For dipping: Marshmallows; chunks of angel food, pound, or sponge cake; whole fresh strawberries; dried fruits; apple chunks; pineapple chunks; pear or peach wedges; mandarin orange segments; banana slices; ice cream balls (prepared beforehand with a melon baller, with a bamboo skewer inserted into each tiny scoop—refreeze until very hard).

PART II

General

SCHOOL DAZE

Options

Ladies' Evening or Luncheon   Back-to-School Celebration (for moms)
School/College Banquet   Teacher Appreciation Banquet

Decorations

Tables   Cover with white paper. Using a felt marker, write simple math equations and words all over (e.g., 2 + 2 = 4, cat, dog, etc.).

Centerpieces   Lay a blue strip of crepe paper down the center of table. Stick a small flag into a shiny red apple, and set several of these down the center of each table.

Program Cover   (See Appendix, Item 2-A.)

Name Tags   (See Appendix, Item 2-B.)

Special Features

Pledge of Allegiance

Prayer

Song   "School Days" (See Resources.)

Games   School photo guessing game (See Resources.)
   Yo-yo contest (See Resources.)
   Jacks (See Resources.)
   Marbles (See Resources.)
   Spelling bee (See Resources.)
   Slang quiz (See Resources.)
   Hopscotch (See Resources.)
   Bible hopscotch (See Resources.)

Math Skit   (See Resources.)

Demonstrations
   Cooking demonstration   Cinnamon candy apples (See Resources.)

Devotional

Invite a guest speaker to talk about building character or self-esteem in children.

Food

Sack lunch ideas (See Resources.)

RESOURCES

School Days

by Will Cobb

School days, school days,
Dear old Golden Rule days.
Readin' and writin' and 'rithmetic,
Taught to the tune of a hickory stick.
You were my queen in calico,
I was your bashful, barefoot beau.
You wrote on my slate, "I love you, Joe,"
When we were a couple of kids.

Games

School photo guessing game   Have each guest submit an old school photo of himself or herself. Post them all on the bulletin board and number them. Guess who's who.

Yo-yo contest   See who can keep his or her yo-yo going longest. You may even have one or two clever people who can do yo-yo tricks.

Jacks   Obtain several sets of jacks with 5 to 10 jacks and a ball in each set. Three to five people can play with each set. Hold all the jacks in the palm of the hand and scatter them on the floor or ground. Throw the ball up in the air; while it is in the air, you pick up one jack and catch the ball after it bounces once. You continue this until you have picked up all the jacks, one at a time, or until you miss either the jack or the ball. If you miss, then it is the next person's turn to try.

If you successfully pick up all the jacks without missing the ball, you then throw the jacks again and pick up two jacks at a time, with the ball, until all are picked up. This continues in increasing increments—picking up three each time, then four, and so on, until all the jacks are picked up on one bounce of the ball. On your next turn you start where you missed on your previous turn. For example, if you missed on two, then start there, or if on five, then start there. The first to pick up all the jacks on one bounce of the ball is the winner.

Marbles   Obtain a large bag of marbles of mixed colors at a variety or toy store. With chalk, draw a circle about 1' in diameter on the ground or floor. Each player puts 3 marbles in the circle. Draw an outer circle 3' to 4' in diameter around the smaller circle. Each player shoots one marble (called a shooter) from the outer circle, trying to knock marbles out of the inner circle. Each player has one shot at a time, and the marbles he knocks out become his.

The player may squat or kneel on one or both knees to obtain the best aiming position. To propel the shooter, the player should balance it in the recess made by the curling of the forefinger around and slightly above the end of the straightened thumb. The player then holds his hand on or close to the ground or floor, takes aim, and flicks his thumb sharply forward to shoot the marble at its target. After each turn, the player retrieves his shooter. The player knocking the most marbles out is the winner.

Spelling bee   Use Bible words or names. Try not to make anyone feel intimidated by this, but have a few really tough words for the smarties.

Slang quiz   Mix up the following slang words and their meanings:

dog cheap (1616)	of little worth
button up (1800s)	be quiet
skedaddle (1800s)	get out of here
short as piecrust (1849)	extremely short-tempered
shutters up (1850s)	keep it secret
skookum (1913)	excellent
wowser (1920s)	good-looking
red lead (1928)	ketchup
copacetic (1933)	satisfactory
egghead (1950s)	smart person
woody (1960s)	wood-paneled station wagon
awesome dude (1990s)	phenomenal character
bad (1990s)	really good

Hopscotch   With chalk, or tape, mark steps from "earth" to "heaven" on the floor or carpet. Make each block 16" to 24" wide. (See diagram.)

General Rules:

Start on earth square and toss a marker to block 1. Hop on one foot from earth to block 1 and back to earth. Toss the marker to block 2, hop to block 2 via block 1, and, standing on one foot, toss the marker back to the earth square. Then hop back to earth square via block 1. Continue doing this by tossing the marker to each block, hopping to that block on one foot, tossing the marker back to earth, and hopping back there. Do this until you reach the heaven square.

If the marker lands on the wrong block, a player lands on the wrong block, or a player steps on the wrong block or puts both feet down, his turn is over. You can stand on both feet in earth and heaven. When it is his turn again, he starts from where he left off. The first player to continue from earth to heaven and back to earth is the winner. If you want to make it harder, you can balance a marker on your head or foot.

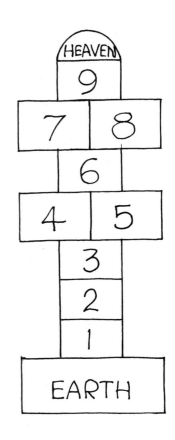

Bible hopscotch   Make two hopscotch tracks on paper, chalkboard, or whiteboard. Choose two teams. Make a list of Bible questions (see suggestions below), some worth one point, some worth two points. The first team to the other end of the hopscotch board is the winner.

Bible hopscotch questions
1. Name the sixth book of the Old Testament. (Joshua)
2. How many days did it rain on Noah? (40)
3. Name the first woman in the Bible. (Eve)
4. (2 points) Name the father of John the Baptist. (Zacharias)
5. Where was Paul from? (Tarsus)
6. Name the book of the Old Testament that tells about creation. (Genesis)

7. Where was Jesus born? (Bethlehem)
8. (2 points) What 2 books have the Ten Commandments? (Exodus and Deuteronomy)
9. (2 points) What book comes after Ezra? (Nehemiah)
10. What was used to feed 5,000 people? (5 loaves and 2 fishes)
11. Who healed 10 lepers? (Jesus)
12. Name a very strong man in the Old Testament. (Samson)
13. Who was sold by his brothers? (Joseph)
14. How many times did Peter deny Christ? (3)
15. (2 points) Name Abraham's wife. (Sarah)
16. Name the mother of John the Baptist. (Elizabeth)
17. Who betrayed Christ? (Judas)
18. Who doubted Christ? (Thomas)
19. (2 points) Where was Paul stoned? (Lystra)
20. Who was king at the time of Jesus' death? (Herod)
21. Who betrayed Samson? (Delilah)
22. (2 points) How many brothers did Joseph have? (11)
23. Name the sons of Noah. (Shem, Ham, and Japheth)
24. What happened to Lot's wife? (She turned into a pillar of salt.)
25. Who received the Old Testament law on a mountain? (Moses)
26. (2 points) What is the shortest book in the Bible? (2 John)
27. (2 points) How many books are in the New Testament? (27)
28. What book comes after Romans? (1 Corinthians)
29. Who was bitten by a snake but did not die? (Paul)
30. (2 points) Who helped the spies in Jericho? (Rahab)

Math Skit

Characters: TEACHER; PUPIL with dunce cap

TEACHER *(writes this problem on the board: 7 x 13 = _____):* Now class, who can solve this problem correctly?

(Before anyone can accept the challenge, the pupil with the dunce cap runs in from the back, shouting.)

PUPIL: I can do it! I can do it! *(Clumsily he grabs the chalk and begins to count on his fingers and toes for a few moments, and then he answers.)* The answer is 28.

TEACHER: How did you arrive at the answer?

PUPIL: Well, 7 times 1 is 7. And I know that 7 times 3 is 21, so *(counting on his fingers again)* 21 plus 7 is 28.

(The TEACHER challenges his wrong answer and makes him check his work, first by division and then by addition. Every time he gets the same answer, so it must be right—even though we know it's wrong. Here is how it's done:)

PUPIL (writes on board: 28 divided by 7 = 13): Seven will not go into 2, so I'll write the 2 (in the palm of his hand) and hold it. Now 7 will go into 8 one time, with 1 left over. If you add the 1 left over with the 2 in your hand, you get 3. Place the 3 next to the 1. That gives you 13. (Write this out in long division.)

TEACHER: No, no, no!

PUPIL: But see: (on board)

```
        13
        13
        13
        13
        13
        13
        13
        ──
        28
```

Start by adding the threes, which add up to 21. Then add the ones to it, bringing the total again to 28. Now who's the dunce?

(At this point the TEACHER throws up her hands in disgust. The PUPIL, laughing, takes his dunce cap off and puts it on the TEACHER's head, and they both go off laughing.)

Sack Lunch Ideas

Here are two sack lunch ideas to choose from, depending upon the type of meeting you are having.

1. Sandwiches, cookies, fruit, canned or boxed drinks—all prepacked in brown paper bags—are given to each person.

2. Each person brings his or her favorite sack lunch and shares it with others. You could also have a bag-decorating contest and see who brings the most cleverly decorated lunch bag.

Cinnamon Candy Apples

These delicious apples are easy to make and are great to take cold in lunches.

Apples	Cream cheese
Cinnamon red-hot candies	Walnuts or pecans

Wash and core apples, and peel a small amount of skin from around the top of the opening. Place in a saucepan with a small amount of water and fill each cavity with red hots. Simmer apples until just tender and all red hots are melted and have made a sauce. Spoon sauce over apples to make them all red. Then pour out excess sauce and set apples and sauce aside to cool. When apples are cool, fill the cavity with a mixture of cream cheese and nuts. Garnish with mint leaves if desired and serve cold with remaining sauce. Delicious in school lunches. Do not overcook.

A PIGMANIA PARTY

Options

Outreach

Teen Party

Women's Ministries Party

Couples' Party

Decorations

Tables   Use purple tablecloths.

Centerpieces   Sandwich boards of pigs. (See Resources.)

Program Cover   (See Appendix, Item 2-C.)

Name Tags   (See Appendix, Item 2-D.)

Pig Snouts   To be worn by hosts/hostesses. (See Resources.)

Special Features

Special Music   Pigtailed women present a selection of music.

Games

Get-acquainted Game

What do you like to *"pig* out" on? (Favorite food)

What do you like to do that is "hog heaven" for you? (Hobbies or sport)

What do you like to *"wallow* in the mire" over? (Pet peeve or something that depresses you)

Pig-a-boo Game

Prepare a bag with several items to look at quickly. Contestants close the bag and try to write down all they saw.

Pigtail Relay

Prepare two boards with three small ropes fastened to them. Two teams compete by running to the boards to braid and unbraid the ropes. Winning team "pigs out" on pork rinds, little sausages in barbecue sauce, and other pork items.

Pig Wit Game

Divide into small groups or couples and make a PIGagraph or a SOW-tence, using a play on words that are pig related.

Illustration:

- Rise and *swine,* even if you didn't get an *oink* of sleep all night.
- It's *sow* crowded in here, I feel like a *sowdine. Piglet* me out!
- You can change words like:

SOWPIGsticated	sophisticated
LOINg	long
STYed	stayed
SWINE	fine, wine, shine
SNOUTshots	snapshots

You can also use words relating to pigs, like *hogwash, hamstring, pigsty, hog, pork,* etc. Set a time limit and then share your pigstorming ideas. The best get the "pig pun" prize (small canned ham, jar of bacon bits, package of bacon, pig refrigerator magnet, sausage biscuit, piggy bank, or jar of pigs' feet).

Demonstrations

Pet Shop   Bring a potbellied pig and tell how it makes a good house pet.

Nursery Rhyme

> *This little piggy went to market—*
> Wise shopping hints for busy families

> *This little piggy stayed home—*
> Hobby or entertainment ideas for all the family

> *This little piggy had roast beef—*
> Ideas for roast beef while living on a hamburger budget

> *This little piggy had none—*
> Diet ideas or ideas on how to do things with nearly nothing

> *This little piggy cried, "Wee, wee, wee," all the way home—*
> Must be a French pig saying, "Yes, yes, yes," all the way home.
> (There are many positive things we can be thankful for.)

Devotional

Read aloud the story of the Three Little Pigs (who built their houses of straw, wood, and brick). Relate it to the wise man who built his house on the rock (Matt. 7:24-27). Option 2: use the lesson of the prodigal son, who found himself in a pig-pen (Luke 15:11-24).

Food

Some Suggested "Pig-out" Menus (choose one or more)

- Bacon, lettuce, and tomato sandwiches
- "Trim pig-out": yogurt and fresh fruit; cottage cheese
- "Pig trough" of aluminum guttering in which to make ice cream sundaes
- Ham sandwiches
- Hot dogs with all the trimmings
- Roast pig on a spit
- Baked ham dinner, with "slopped" (scalloped) potatoes

RESOURCES

Pig Snouts

Enlarge and copy pattern onto flesh-colored paper. Cut out. Cut the curve on the upper (middle) part of the snout, and fold along the dotted line on either side. Gently curve the part extending back so that it will follow the curve of the nose. Attach with double-sided tape to the bridge of the nose. Let the turned-down part of the snout extend over the end of the nose to cover it.

Centerpieces

The sandwich board of pigs is double-sided. Copy the Pigmania program cover design (*see* Appendix, Item 2-C) and tape or glue onto both sides of bright pink posterboard that is cut and folded to fit. Allow extra 2½" for base.

FANTASTIC WOMAN

Options

Women's Meeting   Mother/Daughter Banquet

Decorations

Tables   Cover with different-colored pastel cloths. Use contrasting pastel napkins folded into fan shapes.

Centerpieces   Collect special fans and surround them with a few flowers. (See Appendix, Item 2-E, for fan stand pattern.)

Program Covers and Text Decorations   (See Appendix, Items 2-F and 2-G.)

Name Tags   (See Appendix, Item 2-H.)

Backdrop   A large fan hanging or standing behind the speakers. Option 2: Use several smaller fans hanging from the ceiling.

Special Features

Music   Little singing FANcies (See Resources.)

Contest   FAN making (See Resources.)

History of FANS   (See Resources.)

FANtastic One-Woman Fashion Show   (See Resources.)

Devotional

FANtastic Women Throughout History   (See Resources.)

Food

Light refreshments   FANciful finger food
                                    FANtastic fruit punch

Meal   Beef FANdango (your favorite beef or casserole)
              Emerald FANcies (green vegetables)
              Bread FANS
              FANtasia (fruit salad or light dessert)

RESOURCES

Little Singing FANcies

Young girls in their prettiest pastel dresses sing these words to the tune of "In the Merry, Merry Month of May."

In the merry, merry month of May
We're all coming your way to say,
That to all our moms and grans,
We are still your biggest fans,
And our love for you grows stronger day by day.

FAN-Making Contest

Fill several boxes with various items such as colored paper, printed wrapping paper, glue, ribbon, lace, scissors, etc. Place a box on each table ready for contest. Choose teams. Set a time limit and encourage contestants to make the most creative, beautiful, interesting fan they can from the materials in their boxes. Present gifts (perhaps decorated fans or fan brooches) to the winners.

History of FANS

There are lots of fascinating things to know about the way ladies held their fans in years past. A man's weapon was his sword, but the women had their fans, with which they could make an equally great impression.

Young women of Spain and Europe were taught, through books available in their day, how to express entire sentences with careful actions of their fans. There wasn't a wide scope to the conversation, because it was developed to cover only one vital topic—romance. (Have some women demonstrate the positions of the fan and the interpretations. Then later give a quiz to see how many the audience remembered.) Here are some of the fan positions and their interpretations:

- Placing the fan near the heart: "You have won my heart."
- Clasping the hands under the open fan: "Forgive me."
- Covering the left ear with the open fan: "Do not betray our secret."
- Hiding the eyes behind the open fan: "I love you."
- Shutting the full open fan very slowly: "I promise to marry you."
- Drawing the closed fan across the eyes: "I am sorry."
- Touching the tip of the closed fan with the finger: "I wish to speak to you."
- Dropping the fan: "We will be friends."
- Fanning very slowly: "I am married."
- Fanning very quickly: "I am engaged."
- Opening the fan wide: "Wait for me."
- Placing the fan behind the head: "Do not forget me."
- Carrying the fan in the right hand and in front of the face: "Follow me."
- Carrying the fan in the left hand in front of the face: "I am desirous of your acquaintance."
- Drawing the closed fan across the forehead: "You have changed."
- Twirling the closed fan in the left hand: "We are being watched."
- Twirling the closed fan in the right hand: "I love another."
- Carrying the opened fan in the left hand: "Come and talk to me."
- Presenting the fan shut: "Do you love me?"[1]

---

1. Adapted from Nancy Armstrong, *A Collector's History of Fans* (London: A. M. Heath, 1974), 182-83. The authors and publisher made every effort to locate the owner or the owner's agent for permission to use this material. Appropriate recognition of the copyright holder, if known, will be included in any reprintings.

A FANtastic One-Woman Fashion Show

by Nora Burdett and Karen Keller

Fashion shows are always a hit with women. This is a one-woman show because this lady is the perfect example of the "FANtastic woman." For the audience to really appreciate this model, she must walk around the guests, showing off all her accessories.

Props:

> Kitchen wipe (any color)
> Twist-tie brooch (from loaves of bread)—twist a dozen or so of these together and fasten with a safety pin
> Clothespins made into necklace
> Pinafore apron made from tea towels
> Tape measure
> Wrist pincushion (bracelet)
> White medical jacket
> Thermometer
> Portable phone
> Key ring with several keys
> Megaphone (handbag)
> Gardening gloves (with thumbs painted green)
> Mortarboard (hat)
> Feather duster (decoration for hat)
> Combat or work boots
> Black lace or fishnet stockings
> Fancy garter
> Bottle of perfume
> Expanding photo sheet with photos of herself at different ages and her family
> Bible
> "Wordless Book"
> Small notebook and pencils

Have an emcee use this monologue:

Ladies, thank you so much for coming today to our exclusive showing of this season's FANtastically dressed woman. Our model is none other than the world-famous *(insert model's name)*.

We all know that scarves are in this year. Hers is of the finest kitchen wipe creatively tied around her neck. Her stunning brooch is the latest twist-tie.

With all those "scarves" to wash, we see that she is wearing the laundry's newest design in necklaces—the clothespin look. Charming, isn't it? Useful and environmentally friendly.

We all know that a woman's work is never done, and the best part of that work starts in the kitchen. Fashion is important there, too, so we see she has a pinafore apron that is back in style. It is made of the finest linen tea towels. Every fashion-conscious woman will want one of these this year.

A truly FANtastic woman not only wears designer labels but also is quite handy with the needle and thread herself, as we see by the collector's item accessories such as the tape-measure belt and pincushion bracelet she is wearing.

Today's woman is ready for anything. Her jacket features the medical look, with a special pocket for her thermometer. Every-where she goes she makes temperatures rise. She is never more than a phone call away and has a special pocket in which to house her communication system. She also carries the keys to get every-one where they need to go on time.

Being a sporty woman and an avid supporter of her family and friends, she sports a megaphone handbag, which enables her to cheer them on.

This year gloves are really in. These gloves feature two green thumbs, which are wonderful for making the garden grow.

We are constantly being told nowadays to wear a hat. Look—her choice for the season is the famous mortar-board of the well-ed-ucated and wise woman. Complete with tassel and feather duster, it makes a very clean impression.

One may be impeccably dressed and yet not be comfortable. Our FANtastic woman believes one's feet should be comfortably shod, so she has chosen combat boots, which are not only comfort-able but also protective against life's little battles.

Some FANtastic women are also wonderful wives. Our model has decided to add some spice to her life with black lace stockings and garter. For those special times alone with her husband, she adds a special touch for him, some exotic perfume.

There is little doubt that this model knows just who she is, but if you're in doubt, just take a look at her I.D. *(Model pulls out an ex-panding photo sheet.)* She just happens to have certification of her profession—identity as daughter, sister, wife, and mother (or grand-mother). You may not know her real name, but you doubtless know to whom she belongs—her family.

As executive secretary, she efficiently organizes her office or household. Under her arm she carries the best road map available. Bound in leather with the finest parchment paper pages, she finds it keeps her on the narrow road she desires to travel.

In her pocket she also carries a Wordless Book,* which is useful in helping others, especially little ones, find their way as well. It real-ly does not matter how well-dressed a woman is if she is on the wrong road. Remember: "Man looketh on the outward appearance, but the Lord looketh on the heart" (1 Sam. 16:7).

Susanna
Wesley

Lydia

FANtastic Women Throughout History

Lydia (businesswoman)   Florence Nightingale (nurse)
Susanna Wesley (mother)   Fanny Crosby (songwriter)

Build a 6' x 4' frame covered with lightweight porous fabric (such as cheesecloth), through which characters may be seen. Wings on each side, 6' tall and 2' wide, make it freestanding. The wings can be solid or also covered with cheesecloth. Each participant stands behind the frame with a light placed in front of her. You do not want a silhouette—just the illusion that you are looking back through time. Behind the screen each woman can read her carefully positioned script.

Florence
Nightingale

Fanny
Crosby

*A children's soul-winning tool published by Child Evangelism Fellowship.

LYDIA

Lydia

NARRATOR: We don't know her last name, or even if she was married. But she is an example of a FANtastic businesswoman in history. We are not told whether she was a Jew, but probably she wasn't, since she was from Thyatira in Asia Minor. She had a longing for the truth and had not found it in the worship of Apollo, as many of her countrymen thought they had.

LYDIA: I was a businesswoman, a seller of purple—a well-known cloth imported from my own hometown of Thyatira. I closed my business on the Sabbath and accompanied Jewish women to the place of prayer by the riverside, for there was not a synagogue in Philippi. On one important Sabbath the other women and I were met by a group of men: Paul, Luke, Timothy, and Silas. They had just come from Troas, not because this was where they desired to be, but because the Spirit of God in a vision had prevented them from going elsewhere. And here they found our group of women.

Paul, as was his custom, began to share with us and tell about Jesus Christ, the Messiah for whom we were looking. He had come! Indeed, He would come to release us from our bondage of sin, if only each of us would open our hearts to Him and repent of our sin and accept that He had died for us on the Cross. Paul gave us an opportunity to respond to what he had just told us. That day I believed his words. I believed because the Lord opened my heart. It was not unusual for Jews to reject Him because of the hardness of their hearts.

I was baptized the same day I believed, publicly showing that I believed in the death, burial, and resurrection of Jesus Christ, the Redeemer of my soul. I had to share the news with others and started with my own household. What more important place for a woman to share the gospel than in her own house?[2]

NARRATOR: We know of women who have spent days working for organizations involved in "God's business" while they neglected their husbands and children who were not saved or even sympathetic to the Lord's work. The Lord's work begins at home, and we would all do well to remember that. "She looketh well to the ways of her household" (Prov. 31:27).

Lydia and her household believed and were baptized in obedience to Him. She then opened her home to the men, insisting they stay there for a while. So she began to be a Christian woman of hospitality and, no doubt, continued to share Christ with those in the city of Philippi and all over Macedonia.

(Light goes off for character change.)

2. Adapted from Gien Karssen, *Her Name Is Woman* (Colorado Springs: NavPress, 1975), 187-91. Used by permission of NavPress. All rights reserved.

SUSANNA WESLEY (1669-1742)

Susanna Wesley

NARRATOR: We have chosen to look at the life of Susanna Wesley, an outstanding mother—mother of 19 children (7 of whom died in infancy). Much has been written about Mrs. Wesley, but perhaps the most interesting thing for us to look at today would be her "laws" for rearing children.

SUSANNA: I did not have a perfect home or perfect children. The Bible says, "For all have sinned, and come short of the glory of God" (Rom. 3:23). But I did what I could to bring my children up honestly and lovingly for the Lord. These were my bylaws:

1. Cowardice and fear of punishment often lead children into lying until it becomes a habit with them. Whoever, when found guilty of a crime, would confess it and promise to amend his ways would not be punished.

2. Nothing that was deemed "a sinful action" should go unpunished.

3. If a child mended his ways, he was never to be reminded, chided, or punished for the same fault twice.

4. Good behavior, especially when it came as a result of the child's own inclinations, would be rewarded according to its own merits.

5. If a child obeyed in order to please, the action, though not necessarily done well, was accepted and the child kindly advised how to improve his action the next time.

6. Nothing was ever to be taken from another without his consent.

7. Promises must be strictly observed. Once gifts were given, unless they were conditional and the conditions were broken, they must never be taken back.

8. No girl could be taught to work until she could read. The same amount of time must be spent learning to work as learning to read.[3]

Though these rules seem hard, the age in which we lived was hard. Children were cruelly flogged by wicked schoolmasters. But I always tried to show love for my 12 living children. I believed that "strength guided by kindness" should rule my household, and a special time was set aside for each child every week. When my son John was head of Kingswood School, he employed these methods of teaching and discipline himself.

NARRATOR: Susanna reared her family under extreme poverty. Everything she accomplished was done within a small radius of her home and her husband's parish in Lincolnshire. Yet she gave the world two of the greatest men of all times: John and Charles Wesley.

(Light goes off for character change.)

---

3. Adapted from Rebecca Harmon, *Susanna, Mother of the Wesleys* (Nashville: Abingdon Press, 1968), 61-62. Used with permission.

Florence
Nightingale

FLORENCE NIGHTINGALE (1820-1910)

NARRATOR: Florence Nightingale was born May 12, 1820, in Florence, Italy, and moved to England at the age of five. The product of wealthy Victorian parents, she began early in life to despise the false glitter and glamour of the parties and dances that accompanied their high social standing. She tired of flower arranging, reading, listening to music, and playing games to while away her days. She was attractive, intelligent, and always the center of young men's attention, but there was a serious darkness that seemed to haunt her life. She found herself constantly searching for an answer to it.

FLORENCE: One ray of light shone into my life when my Aunt Hannah first shared the gospel with me. She told me that Jesus Christ had removed the sin barrier between me and God and that to accept what Jesus had done for me would bring contentment here on earth as well as in eternity. However, there was still an aching in my life that came directly from seeing the need for nurses—particularly for the poor. In my day, hospitals were considered dens of iniquity, and only women of ill repute worked in them. Yet, at the age of 17 I felt God had called me to serve Him as a nurse.

There was no place in England to train, and hospital conditions were generally appalling. A war raged within me to do something about both situations. A friend suggested that I study the "Blue Books," which were commission reports on medical services to the poor in London's East End. I not only studied them but also made charts and graphs and registered statistics, which put me at the forefront of understanding hospital management.

I continually battled my family's prejudices against a medical career and tried to persuade them to my way of thinking. However, by the age of 31 I considered my attempt futile and left home to train in Kaiserswerth, Germany. I was disappointed after two years, when I still had not learned the nursing skills I wanted and needed. I had, however, learned much about hospital management and administration, which helped me immensely in later years.

When England and Turkey decided to make war against Russia, I knew my services would be needed on the battlefront. Teamed with 38 handpicked nurses, I left for Crimea, where we had been promised plentiful supplies and marvelous facilities. Instead, we found low morale, pathetic conditions, and precious few supplies. Nevertheless, walking the four miles of corridors with my oil lamp in hand, I determined to demonstrate passion and caring for the wounded that would cause the death rate to decline and the level of morale to increase. We were winning! The soldiers proclaimed us the real heroes of the Crimean War.

From there I went to India, promoting my ideas on sanitation. At the age of 40 I started the Nightingale Training School for Nurses in St. Thomas, the first of its kind. I also advised America on the care of its sick and wounded during the Civil War and was instrumental in the founding of the International Red Cross.

NARRATOR: Florence died at the age of 90, having fulfilled a desire she believed was God-given.[4] Though she was a truly great woman and did much for mankind, there is no evidence that she ever accepted Christ as her personal Savior. No amount of good works will get a person into heaven, because Jesus said, "I am the way, the truth, and the life: no man cometh unto the Father, but by me" (John 14:6).

(Light goes off for character change.)

FANNY CROSBY (1820-1905)

Fanny Crosby

NARRATOR: Fanny was just six weeks old when she was blinded by a medical accident. Her eyes became inflamed from a cold, and her parents called on a doctor other than their own when theirs was not available. The new doctor prescribed the wrong medication, which caused permanent damage to her eyes. By the age of five the prognosis was that she would never see again this side of heaven.

FANNY CROSBY: I disliked being referred to as the "blind hymn writer," and I did not want my accomplishments highlighted because I was blind. I felt a blind person could do nearly anything a sighted person could do.

My earliest recollections are from learning at my mother's and grandmother's knees. Together they prayed that I would have the opportunity to be educated, and God saw to it that the opportunity came. At the age of 15, I left for the New York Institute for the Blind. I was a student there for 8 years and a teacher for 15. At the age of 25 I accepted Jesus Christ as my Lord and Savior during a city revival in New York.

In 1858 I married Alexander Van Alstyne, who had been a fellow student at the institute. He died in 1902. Throughout his life he continually encouraged my hymn writing and even composed the music for several pieces himself. We had a daughter who died in infancy.

NARRATOR: Estimates of how many hymns Fanny wrote are anywhere from 5,000 to 8,000, since it is known that she often used pseudonyms to camouflage her prolific pen. She memorized great portions of the Word of God, especially the Books of the Law and the Gospels. She believed the Bible to be the best reading material in any home and thought that if she could choose the reading material for *every* home, she could save the nation.[5]

---

4. Adapted from Sandy Dengler, *Florence Nightingale: Nurse to Soldiers* (Chicago: Moody Press, 1988), 131-36. Used by permission.

5. Adapted from Blanche Gosselin, "She Hath Done What She Could," *Fundamentalist Journal,* May 1988, 23-27. Used by permission of Old Time Gospel Hour, Lynchburg, Va.

PATCHWORK OF MEMORIES

Options

Church Anniversary Program   Mother/Daughter Banquet
Outreach

Decorations

Tables   Cover with pink cloths.

Centerpieces   Oil lamps or candles and breadbaskets filled with dried breadsticks, rolls, and slices in various sizes and shapes. (See Resources.)

Program Covers   (See Appendix, Item 2-I.) Cut small pieces of fabric and paste into the sections of each program cover, or copy the design provided.

Name Tags   (See Appendix, Item 2-J.)

Walls and Room   Use a clean old wooden ladder (or more than one, depending on the size of the room) and hang several quilts on various rungs for decoration. Accent with a few green plants.

Special Features

Background Music   Set the mood by using music box, player piano, or harpsichord music. Recordings are available at music stores.

Game   Quilting Fabric Quiz (See Resources.)

Photo Booth   Set up "Ye Olde Photo Shoppe" to look like an old parlor with cane rocking chair, hatstand, and shawls. Drape a small round table with a long lace tablecloth to hold an old-fashioned framed picture and an old Bible with a pair of antique glasses on it. Take small-group photos. You may need to make a slight charge for film and processing.

Poem   "Patchwork of Life" (See Resources.)

Reading   "The Meanest Mother in the World" (See Resources.)

Skit   "Walnuts or Popcorn" (See Resources.)

Bulletin Board   (See Resources.)

Church Anniversary   (See Resources.)

Devotional

The Patchwork Quilt   (See Resources.)

Food

Pink punch
Sandwiches—ribbon, checkerboard, and pinwheel (See Resources.)
Petits fours or cupcakes

RESOURCES

Dried Bread Centerpieces

Variety of bread: rolls, slices, small loaves, bread sticks, and so on
Clear spray varnish (gloss)
Baskets (wicker paper plate holders suggested)
Fine wire
Hot glue and glue gun
Patchwork-printed ribbon
Dried flowers or wheat

Dry bread in oven at 150° degrees for 8 to 10 hours. Cool. Spray with clear varnish. Using wicker paper plate baskets, hot glue the bread, ribbons, and wheat or flowers in pleasing arrangements. These will lie on the tables as centerpieces. Attach a small wire loop to the back of each basket so that they can be hung on the wall, since you may want to offer these for sale after your program.

Ribbon Sandwiches

1 loaf unsliced wheat bread
1 loaf unsliced white bread
¼ cup butter or margarine
Choice of fillings (listed below)
Choice of garnishes (listed below)

Trim crusts from unsliced loaves. Slice lengthwise into ½" slices.

Lightly butter one long slice white bread and spread with thin layer of filling (as suggested below). Avoid coarse or dry fillings for this. Top with a slice of wheat bread and repeat process until you have used 4 slices. Put no filling on outside slices. Wrap entire loaf in plastic wrap and refrigerate for at least 1 hour before cutting into ½" slices and serving.

Variation: Entire assembled loaf can be "frosted" with light cream cheese. Mix cream cheese with 2 tablespoons milk and spread over entire loaf. Use garnishes as mentioned below. Cut into 1" slices and eat with a fork.

Fillings or spreads: Tuna salad, egg salad, pimento cheese, avocado/cream cheese, ham salad, deviled ham, cream cheese/chives, cream cheese/walnuts, liverwurst, or paté.

Garnishes: Sliced stuffed or black olives, mushroom slices, anchovies, fresh dill or parsley, pimento, radish slices, sweet pickle slices, shredded cheese, egg or cucumber slices, caviar. Garnishes add color and sparkle.

Checkerboard Sandwiches

1 ribbon loaf
butter or margarine
filling (optional)

Cut assembled ribbon loaf described above into ½" slices. Spread soft butter or margarine on 1 slice. Top with second slice, placing the dark

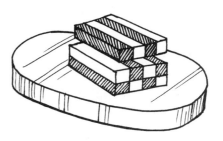

strip on top of the light one. Press together gently but firmly. Spread margarine or butter on second slice; top with a third slice with the light strip on top of the dark. Press together gently but firmly. Wrap in plastic wrap and refrigerate for at least 1 hour. Cut into ½" slices and serve.

Variation: Instead of using butter or margarine between layers, spread thinly with avocado/cream cheese or deviled ham.

Pinwheel Sandwiches

> 1 unsliced loaf of bread
> butter or margarine
> choice of filling

Trim the crust from an unsliced loaf of bread. Slice lengthwise into ¼" slices. Spread each long slice with 2 tablespoons of butter or margarine and ½ cup of one of the suggested fillings.

Cut each long slice crosswise into halves. Roll up tightly, beginning at narrow end. Secure with wooden picks. Wrap in plastic wrap and refrigerate for 1 hour. Cut each roll into slices about ½" thick.

Variation: Pita bread (single layer) or flour tortillas may be used instead of unsliced loaf.

Quilting Fabric Quiz

1. A used chair	A. felt
2. A string and a boy's name	B. checked material
3. Babies like to untie these	C. red material
4. To gain a profit	D. satin
5. A tall tale	E. print material
6. Sunday afternoon ride	F. flannel outing
7. Find this in a book	G. ribbons
8. Find this in a bank	H. corduroy
9. Has been touched	I. net
10. Roses are _ _ _	J. yarn

Answers:

1—D	2—H	3—G	4—I	5—J
6—F	7—E	8—B	9—A	10—C

Patchwork of Life

(Author Unknown)

Life's not all light and sunshine,
　　Nor is it all joy and cheer.
For each has his share of worries,
　　His share of doubt and fear.
Seems that life's just a pattern
　　Like the patches on a quilt.
And bits of shade and sunshine
　　Are the squares from which we're built.
All the sunshine squares are pretty,
　　While the shadow ones are plain.
But you know how much brighter
　　Is the sunshine after rain.

And you know that the pretty patches
    Simply never would be seen,
Were it not for all the plain ones
    Sewn so neatly in between.[1]

The Meanest Mother in the World

(Author Unknown)

I have the meanest mother in the whole world. While other kids eat candy for breakfast, I have to have cereal, eggs, or toast. When other kids have Cokes and chips for lunch, I have to have a high-protein sandwich. As you might guess, my dinner is different from theirs too. But at least I am not alone in my suffering. My brother has the same mean mother as I do.

My mother insists on knowing where we are at all times. You'd think we were on a chain gang. She has to know who our friends are and what we are doing. If we say we'll be gone for an hour, she insists that it is not a hour and five minutes. We can't sleep till noon like our friends. In fact, my mother is so mean that she breaks child labor laws by making us work. We have to wash dishes and make beds, learn to cook and do all sorts of exhausting jobs. I believe she lies awake at night thinking up mean things to do to us.

She always insists on our telling the truth, the whole truth, and nothing but the truth, even if it kills us—and sometimes it nearly does.

Now that we are teenagers our lives are becoming even more unbearable. There is none of this tooting of the car horn for us to come running. She embarrasses us to no end by making our friends come to the door to get us, and she says she will insist on the same behavior from our dates one day. And speaking of dating—while our friends are dating by 13 or 14, my mean mother has refused to let us start dating until we are at least 17. Seventeen, that is! And we can only go to a church or school function, then straight home.

As you can easily see, my mother is a complete failure. None of us has ever been arrested or sent to juvenile court. We haven't experimented with drugs or sex. We don't hang around the shops with the other kids in the neighborhood who have nothing to do, and we have never thought of running away from home. And who do we have to blame? That's right. Our mean mother. She is literally forcing us to grow up into God-fearing, educated, honest adults.

It is with this background that I look forward one day to being a mother. Then, when my children call me mean, I will stand a little taller and be filled with pride. You see, I can thank God for the meanest mother in the whole world, and I want to be just like her.[2]

Walnuts or Popcorn

by Karen Keller

NARRATOR: Mother is in the attic of her elderly parents' home. Her

---

1. Prepared by Evelyn Miles in "Patchwork" for Christian Women Communicating Intl. in Australia, Strathfield, New South Wales. Used with permission.

2. The authors and publisher made every effort to locate the owner or the owner's agent for permission to use this material. Appropriate recognition of the author and copyright holder, if known, will be included in any reprintings.

mother has Alzheimer's disease and has just been put into a nursing home because her family is unable to care for her adequately. The family home is to be sold soon, so everything must be sorted and divided, sold, or done away with. The teenage DAUGHTER is helping, though she would rather be doing something else.

MOTHER: Oh, all this has been so hard—I never realized my folks had so many things stored up here. This has already taken weeks, and I'm having a hard time deciding what needs to be kept and what needs to be sent to charity or thrown away.

DAUGHTER: Well, I think we should just call Goodwill to come and get everything in this attic. Then I could go to Jessica's slumber party instead of being stuck with this mess all weekend.

MOTHER: Many of the things up here were my mother's when she was a girl or newly married. This old trunk is full of things that were special to her through the years. You might find sorting them interesting.

DAUGHTER: Well, I don't see how. Grandma hasn't known me since I was six, and I hardly feel I know her. Ever since I can remember, she has been forgetting things and losing things out of her purse. Whenever we leave her, even for a minute, she drives us crazy by getting lost.

MOTHER: I am so sorry you never really got to know your grandmother. She was a lovely, interesting woman and a very good mother to me as I grew up. She was a good wife and a Christian who lived and shared what she believed.

DAUGHTER (opens trunk—finds a scrapbook, a hankie, a box of newspaper clippings, and some other items): Look at this hankie! It has "France" written on it. What would Grandma be doing with a hankie from France?

MOTHER: That was sent to her by her boyfriend, who went away during the Second World War and was killed.

DAUGHTER: Really? You mean Grandma had a boyfriend who was not Grandpa?

MOTHER: Yes, she was really a beautiful young lady, and there were several young men interested in her.

DAUGHTER: Wow! Look at these old pictures. Who was that?

MOTHER: That was your grandmother when she was a teenager. You look a lot like her.

DAUGHTER: I guess with a bathing suit like that they never had to worry about getting too much sun. I really *do* look like her, don't I? Hey—look at these old cardboard records!

MOTHER: Yes, your grandmother said that each week a new cardboard record was sold with the latest hit song on it. This one was on sale and she bought it for 20 cents. That was big money back then.

DAUGHTER: Look at these old newspaper clippings. Was that really my grandmother's wedding story? She was beautiful! It says the bridesmaids wore organdy dresses with flowers embroidered in wool thread. That sounds really different. Wow—here's your birth announcement! It's hard to believe my mom was ever a baby. Look at this front-page clipping—"Harold Wilcox Sent to Prison for Embezzlement." Who was *he?*

MOTHER: He was your grandmother's brother and my uncle. I will tell you all about him later. He was the black sheep of the family.

DAUGHTER: This old clipping of recipes is about to fall apart. This looks like your recipe for cranberry sauce that you said your mother always made. Our old family recipe started out as a newspaper recipe. Think of that! Look at this one. It's out of the women's page of our church paper back in 1943. I didn't know our church did a monthly paper way back then.

MOTHER: It was probably even more important then, because there was no TV nor as much printed material, especially for women.

DAUGHTER: Listen to what it says: "We have been talking about 'victory gardens' and 'home canning' for several weeks now. This month we are going to deal with some different aspects of life relating to the theme of canning." What was a "victory garden"?

MOTHER: Because of the Second World War, much of our food was being sent overseas to help our troops fight. Our country encouraged everyone to grow a garden. So, many people dug up flower beds and grew vegetables, and then canned them to help the nation's food supply. Growing gardens and canning was time-consuming and something of a new experience for many already busy women. Our gasoline was rationed, as well as sugar and many other things.

DAUGHTER: Things were really different back then.

MOTHER: Yes, they were. But many of the problems were the same ones women face today. I think you will see what I mean if you read a little farther.

DAUGHTER *(continues to read article):* "Think of a canning jar as a day into which only so much can be packed. In canning you pack the container firmly and solidly with the fruit, vegetables, or meat and then add the liquid to fill every bit to within ½ inch of the top. We would be unwise if we filled the jar with liquid first and then tried to pour in the fruit or vegetables to be canned. This can be applied to our activities in a day. Let's pretend that walnuts represent the important things that need to be done, and popcorn as those things less important. Many times we fill our jar with popcorn and then don't have any room for the walnuts. Decide what your walnuts are and put them in the jar, and then add the popcorn. You will be surprised how much popcorn you can pack around the walnuts. The world war has forced us to add more walnuts." *(She stops reading and speaks to her mother.)* Mother, this article is really about priorities, isn't it? I thought this was a new problem because of our fast pace of life.

MOTHER: It has *always* been a problem. Satan has always wanted us to fill our jars with popcorn and not have any room for our walnuts. It has always been hard to see the difference between walnuts and popcorn in our lives. That's why it was in the church paper. Let's try this. There's a bag of leftover popcorn from last night down in the kitchen, and I saw some walnuts in a bowl in the dining room. Why don't you go down and get them?

(DAUGHTER exits and returns with popcorn and walnuts. There is a box of canning jars beside the trunk. They fill a jar with popcorn and try to add walnuts. It does not work. They put in walnuts first and then most of the popcorn is fitted in around the walnuts by shaking the jar.)

MOTHER: That principle really is true.

DAUGHTER: The hard part is deciding what's a walnut and what's popcorn. I guess the walnuts are different for everyone, and they change at different stages in life.

MOTHER: Well, that's somewhat true, but some walnuts are always walnuts, because God's Word says they are always important. *(Here add whatever you want to emphasize, or if this if given at a special time of year or on a special day, you can emphasize the proper values of that season or day.)* Spending time daily with the Lord in His Word and in prayer are always very important. Family responsibilities are always walnuts. Husbands, wives, and children have responsibilities, and it's important they be given priority. Families need to help each other and follow God's plan. Many people today take these responsibilities very lightly.

DAUGHTER: Another walnut is proper attitude. I guess I had some trouble seeing that helping you finish sorting Grandma's things was a walnut, and the slumber party I missed was just popcorn. You know, Mom, this is an important job. I'm glad I came along to help, even if at first I gave you lots of trouble and didn't have a good attitude about it. I've learned a lot about my grandmother today. I want to keep a lot of these clippings to share Grandma's memory with my kids someday. Families are important, and Grandma was an interesting person. Mom, as a teenager it really is hard sometimes to get priorities straight when your friends are pressing you to go along with them. Pray with me that I don't lose sight of what's really a walnut and what's only popcorn.

MOTHER: Always getting my priorities right is hard for me too. *(MOTHER and DAUGHTER hold hands and bow their heads.)* Dear Heavenly Father, we thank You that You are always with us helping us to do what is pleasing to You. Both of us struggle with deciding what the real priorities are. Please help Beth stay close to You and be discerning about how she spends her time. And I need Your guidance as I put walnuts in *my* jar. Thank You for this special time we have shared today as mother and daughter. In Jesus' name, Amen.

DAUGHTER: Well, a priority right now is eating. Let's crack these walnuts and eat them with the popcorn.

MOTHER *(with a big smile on her face):* Now I wonder how *that* fits into this discussion!

Bulletin Board

This is an effective way to carry out your theme. Use old calendars with pictures of quilt blocks or patterns placed around the edge of the bulletin board as a border. You could also use pages from an old wallpaper catalog. In the center on a plain background put one of these messages:

1. A Patchwork of Memories
2. When your world falls apart, let God's love patch it together

Church Anniversary

Create a bulletin board or memory book with "Past Patches of the Church Quilt," which features the founding pastor, other previous pastors, outstanding events, and pictures of the church's history.

The devotion or message could be titled "The Patch *Work* of the Church," featuring the purpose and ministries of the church. In advance, each family could be given a square of muslin to decorate with their name, and these could be made into a quilt. As an alternative, use a smooth tablecloth and have each family sign their name. Either of these could be presented to the pastor or church.

The Patchwork Quilt

Patchwork quilting is experiencing a renaissance today, not so much for necessity's sake, but for the sheer joy of the craft. There are some lessons for us in the patchwork quilt.

1. *Quilts are handmade.*

   We, too, are specially handmade by God. Job said, "Thine hands have made me and fashioned me . . ." (Job 10:8). And the Psalmist said as well, "Thy hands have made me and fashioned me" (Ps. 119:73).
2. *Quilts are purposefully designed.*

   Our purpose is to glorify God (1 Cor. 6:20).
3. *Quilts are filled with batting, which makes them usable.*

   The Christian must remain filled with the Holy Spirit—daily, hourly, moment by moment—in order to be most useful (Rom. 8:9; Eph. 5:18).

AUSTRALIAN BUSH BARBECUE

Options

Teachers'/Workers' Banquet   Father/Son Banquet

All-Church Banquet   Missions Banquet

Decorations

Tables   Use white tablecloths and brown napkins.

Centerpieces   Kerosene lamps and/or folded paper kangaroos and koalas. (See Resources.)

Program Covers   (See Appendix, Items 2-K and 2-L.*)

Name Tags   (See Appendix, Item 2-M.)

Walls   Obtain pictures and posters of Australia from a travel agent.

*The program cover uses the term "bar-be," the Australian equivalent of "barbecue."

Special Features

Games

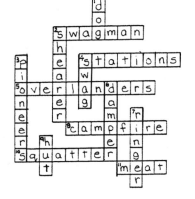

    Bush fire brigade   Almost every rural Australian town has its own fire brigade, which is usually manned by volunteers. It is responsible for extinguishing fires in the community. Make this a relay race in which teams transport buckets of "water" from a container at one end of the room to a container at the other end. (You could use bits of Styrofoam peanuts instead of water.) The first team to fill their container wins.

    Kangaroo relay   Divide into teams. Each player holds an object between his knees and jumps along to the turnaround line and back to the start. The player may not hold the object in place with his hand. The object may be a block of wood, a pillow, or a balloon.

    Crossword   (See Appendix, Item 2-N. Solution at left.)

    Shooting contest   Compete against each other by shooting Styrofoam cups off sawhorses with water pistols or rubber band guns.

    Awards/Certificates   (See Resources.)

Devotional

    On the Australian coat of arms is an emu and a kangaroo. These animals were chosen for their inability to go backward. As Christians, we are encouraged by Paul to be diligent in "forgetting those things which are behind, and reaching forth unto those things which are before, . . . press[ing] toward the mark for the prize of the high calling of God in Christ Jesus" (Phil. 3:13-14).

Food

Menu (See Appendix, Item 2-O.)

Tonight's Tucker

Roast Jumbuck	Lamb or beef
Roast Spuds	Potatoes
"Sturt's Desert" Peas	Green peas
Gravy	
Damper* and Cockey's Joy	Bread and syrup
Shearer's Delight	Pavlova*
Billy Tea and Coffee	

*Recipes in Resources.

RESOURCES

Centerpieces

1. *Kangaroo* (See Appendix, Item 2-P.) Copy kangaroo pattern onto folded brown construction paper, with fold of paper serving as kangaroo's back. Cut out figure, but do not cut on fold. Turn tail up by folding on the dotted lines so that it sticks up and out. Glue head together, pressing ears apart. Put ends of pouch to back of fold at lower-leg level and glue.

2. *Koala* (See Appendix, Item 2-Q.) Enlarge koala to 5½" tall. Cut koala out of gray construction paper. Fold arms and legs forward so that figure will stand.

Awards/Certificates

(See Appendix, Item 2-R.) For special awards, the merit certificate could be given to appropriate guests. Simply copy the design in the Appendix. You will need to explain what each award means. The reason for giving the merit award, as well as an explanation of it, follows:

Treacle Award—For someone who sticks to the stuff and stays sweet about it. (Also known as "cockey's joy," treacle is a sweet, dark, thick, syrupy substance much like molasses—only sweeter. It is used a lot in Australian cooking.)

Old Digger Award—For being the oldest member and faithfully supporting the ministry of the church. (A digger is a soldier, and an "old digger" refers to an ex-soldier.)

Drover's Award—For faithfully rounding up the lambs for Sunday School and getting them into the paddocks (pens) on time on Sundays. (This award could be given to the Sunday School bus driver. A drover is one who drives sheep or cattle to market or from property to property. He might also be referred to as an "overlander.")

Kelpie Award—For being the best friend in Sunday School. (You've heard that the dog is man's best friend. The kelpie is the beloved Australian sheepdog and especially loves a romp with children as well as the sheep on the station. This award could be given to a favorite Sunday School teacher.)

Old Snagger Award—For all the loving work put into the senior citizens' ministry. (Here's a great award to present to the person who works with older folks. A snagger is an old-timer.)

Jackaroo Award—For being one of the young people in training as well as caring for our young people. (The jackaroo is the young stockman who has recently come to work on the station. The young person receiving this award could be a youth worker or student worker.)

Overseer Award—For ably managing the organizing of our meal tonight. (An overseer is the manager of the station. There just isn't much he can't do. He would not normally do the cooking, but he would hire and fire the cooks and other workers on the station. Cooks are precious commodities on the stations, so they have to be treated well, even if they aren't too great.)

Jolly Jumbuck—For one we don't see a lot of, but whom we enjoy when we do. (A jumbuck is a sheep. This could be a person who would love to be at church more often but is hindered by his or her job or another reason. The winner should be someone who is jolly and fun to be around.)

Squatter's Award—For fair and loving management of the sheep of this station. Thanks for feeding us so well! (The squatter is the landowner, the headman. This award is excellent to give to your pastor. While we know that Christ is the Head of the Church, we all value our pastors' leadership, wisdom, and counsel. The squatter's boundaries are limited only by his vision, because he can claim the land for as far as he can see. Thank God for a pastor with vision, for "Where there is no vision, the people perish" [Prov. 29:18].)

Pavlova

4 egg whites	Pinch salt
1 cup sugar	1 teaspoon vinegar
½ teaspoon vanilla	1 tablespoon cornstarch

Beat whites of eggs with salt five to six minutes. Gradually add sugar, vinegar, and vanilla. Beat until stiff. Sift in cornstarch and fold in lightly. Dampen an ovenproof plate, about 12" in diameter, and heap mixture in center. (Do not grease plate.)

Using an electric oven: Preheat to 400° F. Place pavlova in oven, immediately setting oven at 250° F. Bake undisturbed 1½ hours—no longer.

Using gas oven: Bake 10 minutes at 400° F. Then lower to about 200-250° F. for 1 hour.

Top cooled pavlova with whipped cream and decorate with fresh or canned fruits as desired. Strawberries, bananas, kiwi, passion fruit, peaches, and pineapple are favorites in Australia.

Damper

3 cups self-rising flour (or plain flour + 1 teaspoon baking powder per cup)
1½ teaspoon salt
6 tablespoons butter or margarine
½ cup milk (or buttermilk)
½ cup water
Extra flour

Sift flour and salt into bowl. Rub or cut in butter until mixture resembles fine bread crumbs, fairly even in size. Make a well in center of dry ingredients and add combined water and milk all at once. Mix lightly with sharp knife in cutting motion. Turn onto lightly floured surface. Knead lightly. Knead dough into round ball and place on greased oven tray or cookie sheet. Pat dough into a 6" circle. With sharp knife, cut two slits across dough like a cross, approximately ½" deep. Brush top of dough with milk, and sift a little extra flour over dough. Bake in hot oven 10 minutes or until golden brown. Reduce heat to moderate and cook 15 minutes more. Damper does not keep or freeze well, so for best flavor make and eat it on the same day. Serve with butter and "cockey's joy" (dark corn syrup will do).

EVENING IN HOLLAND

Options

Women's Outreach   Missions Program
Mother/Daughter Outreach

Decorations

Tables   Use blue tablecloths and white napkins.

Centerpieces   Potted tulips

Program Cover   (See Appendix, Item 2-S or 2-T.)

Name Tags   (See Appendix, Item 2-U.)

Backdrop   (See Appendix, Item 2-S.)

Walls   Travel posters of Holland/the Netherlands (Contact your local travel agent.)

Special Features

Music   Dutch boy and girl singing "Will You Marry Me?" (See Resources.)

Game   Dutch Shopping List (See Resources.)

Film Video   Travel film or video on Holland (Check with your local library.)

Devotional

1. Dikes—Christ died to reclaim you for His own.
2. Royal Delft Blue Pottery—You should show the marks of a true Christian through an obedient life.
3. Tulips—You should grow so that God can use you to see His life reproduced in others.

(See Resources for all three.)

Food

Dutch cheeses (Gouda, Edam, Kernhem, Bluefort, Leiden)

Platters of cold meats

Pickled herring (an old Dutch favorite). Available in imported sections of specialty food stores and delicatessens. May also be ordered by supermarkets.

Crackers

Yeast breads

Apple tarts (See Resources.)

Crystal cookies (See Resources.)

RESOURCES

Will You Marry Me?

To the tune of "Did You Ever See a Lassie?" Two people hold up Dutch boy and girl masks as they sing (See Appendix, Items 2-V and 2-W).

Cast Dutch BOY
      Dutch GIRL
      CHANTERS (three to four people)

GIRL: Oh, I'm a little Dutch girl, a Dutch girl, a Dutch girl.
      Oh, I'm a little Dutch girl; a Dutch girl I am.

BOY: Oh, I'm a little Dutch boy, a Dutch boy, a Dutch boy,
      Oh, I'm a little Dutch boy; a Dutch boy I am.

TOGETHER: Go this way and that way and this way and that way.

GIRL: Oh, I'm a little Dutch girl; a Dutch girl I am.
      (Spoken chant)
      Oh, Dutch boy, Dutch boy, won't you marry me with your hair so
         golden blond?

BOY *(spoken chant)*:
      Oh, no, sweet maid—I cannot marry you,
      for I have no pants to put on. *(Turns around to show patches.)*

CHANTERS *(spoken chant)*:
      So up she went to her grandfather's chest
      and brought him some *pants* of the very, very best.
      She brought him some *pants* of the very, very best,
      and the Dutch boy put them on. *(To quickly change from his old
         look to his new look, he steps behind a screen and pulls off
         the old patches, which are secured by tape or spray adhe-
         sive.)*

CHORUS

GIRL: Oh, I'm a little Dutch girl, a Dutch girl, a Dutch girl.
      Oh, I'm a little Dutch girl; a Dutch girl I am.

BOY: Oh, I'm a little Dutch boy, a Dutch boy, a Dutch boy.
      Oh, I'm a little Dutch boy; a Dutch boy I am.

TOGETHER: Go this way and that way and this way and that way.

GIRL: Oh, I'm a little Dutch girl; a Dutch girl I am.
      (Spoken chant)
      Oh, Dutch boy, Dutch boy, won't you marry me
      with your hair so golden blond?

BOY: Oh, no, sweet maid—I cannot marry you,
      for I have no socks to put on. *(Shows a sock with a toe peeping
         out.)*

CHANTERS: So up she went to her grandfather's chest . . .
(Continue song, inserting items of clothing in verses, re-
peating chorus between each.)
For I have no shoes to put on.
For I have no shirt to put on.
For I have no coat to put on.
For I have no hat to put on.
For I have me a wife of my own!

(GIRL chases BOY off stage.)

Dutch Boy and Girl Masks

Copy patterns from Appendix, Items 2-V and 2-W, and transfer to sturdy white cardboard. Paint features on; cut out eyes. Attach a small rod behind the cardboard for character to use in holding mask in front of face.

Shopping List

Mix up the list of Dutch words and have participants match the foods to their Dutch names.

WHAT DO I NEED?	WAT HEB IK NODIG?
Potatoes (Earth Apples)	*Aardappelen*
Bread	*Brood*
Butter	*Boter*
Biscuit	*Beschuit*
Eggs	*Eieren*
Vegetables	*Groente*
Honey	*Honing*
Jam	*Jam*
Cheese	*Kaas*
Cocoa	*Cacao*
Coffee	*Koffie*
Matches	*Lucifers*
Flour	*Meel*
Milk	*Melk*
Mustard	*Mosterd*
Oil	*Olie*
Pepper	*Peper*
Rice	*Rijst*
Soap	*Soep*
Tea	*Thee*
Sugar	*Suiker*
Onions	*Uien*
Meat	*Vlees*
Fish	*Vis*
	(Pronounce V as F)

Devotional

Three aspects of Dutch life:

1. Dikes

"The Netherlands" means "lowlands." Holland is unique in that much of its land is swampy and lies below sea level. But the hearty, hardworking, persistent Dutch have taken this "useless" land and made it profitable by reclaiming it from the sea, using dikes. Christ reclaimed us for His own by dying for us. See Rom. 3:23, 10, 12; Eph. 2:8-9; Isa. 51:1; and Ps. 40:1-4.

2. Royal Delft Blue Pottery

Every pottery manufacturer puts his own identifying mark on his work. Through the ages, forgers have tried to copy the work of the masters, including those at Royal Delft. In Delft several factories produced cheap copies of Royal Delftware. Their factory marks were so close to the original that many have been fooled into believing they were getting authentic pieces. Today the casual tourist collecting curios from Holland might pick up any blue-and-white china or pottery, not realizing or caring that it is only a cheap copy of the real thing.

This is true with Christianity as well. God's Word warns us of many false teachers and false religions who may incorporate some truth with their lies. The marks of the true Christian that God's Word tells us to look for are:

    a. Salvation—Eph. 2:8-9; Acts 4:12

    b. Obedience to God—John 8:31; 7:17; 5:21; 2 Tim. 3:15-17; Titus 2:1; John 14:15; 1 John 5:3

    c. Love the brethren—John 13:34-35; 1 John 3:14; Gal. 6:10

3. Tulips

Developing new varieties and improving quality as well as mass production is a very complex and time-consuming business. One interesting thing is the way a stock is multiplied. It's not done from seed but from the bulb itself. This is done so that characteristics of the new bulbs will be identical to those of the original.

This form of reproduction is done by removing the flower (this is called "heading") so that the bulb can use all its energy for its own growth. As the months progress, a new shoot or two may develop inside the bulb beside the original. This actually forms a new bulb called a "bulbil." These bulbils are peeled off by hand, planted, and grow to form complete bulbs. The next year they in turn produce bulbils. As you can see, this reproduction is time-consuming but very reliable.

In the spiritual realm, the Christian or child of God is encouraged to reproduce himself. This can be done only as we put our energy into sharing the gospel (1 Cor. 9:19-22). This will produce new Christians much like the headed tulip bulb produces bulbils. "Heading" in the Christian life would be denying ourselves of time-consuming, selfish interests and devoting our energies to reaching others (Prov. 11:30).

Apple Tarts

Dough:
1⅞ cups flour
2 teaspoons baking powder
½ cup + 1 tablespoon sugar
1 egg white (save yolk for glazing top)

Mix all ingredients together into even dough, roll out, and separate in half. Lay one half on baking sheet. Leave other half for top.

Filling:
8 apples   ½ cup sugar
1 teaspoon cinnamon   Mixed dried fruit

Grate apples. Mix in sugar or sprinkle on top. Place on top of dough. Sprinkle with cinnamon and fruit. Cut remaining half of dough into strips and arrange on top. Glaze with egg yolk mixed with ¾ cup milk. Bake at 350° F. for 1 hour and 15 minutes.

Crystal Cookies

¼ pound butter or margarine
1 cup flour
½ cup sugar
Sugar crystals

Egg white
1 teaspoon mixed spice
1 teaspoon cinnamon

Mix butter, flour, sugar, and spices together. Spread on baking sheet. Brush with egg white and sprinkle on sugar crystals. Bake in oven until brown. Cut while warm, and leave until cool enough to eat.

GOD GAVE THE SONG

Options

Choir Banquet   All-Church Banquet   Outreach

Decorations

Tables   Use white tablecloths with one strip of black crepe paper flat along the middle of the table with red napkins.

Centerpieces   On the black strips set white bud vases, each with a red rose, some greenery, and baby's breath.

Program Covers   Use red paper. (See Appendix, Items 2-X and 2-Y.)

Name Tags   (See Appendix, Item 2-Z.)

Bulletin Boards   (See Resources.)

Special Features

Piano Duet   "Practice Makes Perfect." This piece, by Ernie and Debby Rettino, is available by contacting your local Christian bookstore.

Game   "Name That Gospel Tune." Have someone play a few bars of a familiar hymn. The first person who stands and reveals the correct hymn title receives a gift.

Quiz   Music Quiz (See Resources.)

Theme Song   "God Gave the Song" by Bill and Gloria Gaither. You will need a narrator and a pianist-singer to perform the song.

Devotional

"What Is Music?" (See Resources.) Option 2: Show a film on Fanny Crosby (check your local library or Christian bookstore).

Food

Harmony steak (baked steak in gravy)

Percussion potatoes (mashed potatoes)

String beans (green beans)

Drum roll (dinner rolls with butter)

Sweet melody (dessert)

Finale (coffee, tea, and mints)

Provide live music with dinner if possible. Use piano, harp, cello, violin, and/or flute.

RESOURCES

Bulletin Boards

1. Back the bulletin board with red cloth and border it in black with black silhouettes of musical instruments—with the words "Make a Joyful Noise unto the Lord."

2. Use a white background trimmed in a double-scalloped edge of black over red. Use these words:

> The Lord Is
> My Strength
> and My Song
> and Is Become My Salvation

Use treble clefts in place of the S's. The remainders of the words, -trength, -ong, and -alvation, are done in red. All the rest, including the treble clefs, are done in black.

Music Quiz

Mix up the answers to these terms and names, and have people draw a line from the term to its definition and from the names to the songs written.

Accent	Emphasize
Allegretto	Lively
Andante	Graceful
Animato	Animated; excited
Coda	End; tailpiece
Crescendo	Getting louder
Dolce	Sweet; soft
Encore	An extra piece
Forte	Loud
Fortissimo	Very loud
Furioso	Wildly
Mezzo Forte	Half loud
Pianissimo	Very soft
Staccato	Detached; shortened
Fanny Crosby	Blessed Assurance
John W. Peterson	Surely Goodness and Mercy
Charles Wesley	Christ the Lord Is Risen Today

What Is Music?

Music is a composition of harmony and melody. Musical notes on their own have value but no purpose. It is only when they are placed into a relationship with the right musical staff that they begin to have some significance. Just as a composer must be able to put the right note in the right place for it to be useful, so God has a place and purpose for each of us.

The melody is the chief theme of a musical composition. Harmony is a succession of chords that blend or agree with the melody to make an even more pleasant sound. We need to agree with Him that in His sight we are all sinners prior to salvation and that we need to accept His payment for our sin. This adds the harmony of God's forgiveness and fellowship to our lives.

When several notes are combined to form different tones, we call these chords. There are two types of chords: major and minor. Major chords are positive, depicting joy and happiness. Minor chords depict sadness, depression, and sorrow. Life is full of both major and minor chords—happiness and sadness. In the long run it isn't nearly as important what chords run through the song of our lives, but rather our reaction to those chords.

The rest is a fairly small sign in written music. Rests are very important—without them, music would have little appeal, no beauty, no pauses between an endless string of sounds. Rests are little breaks that give us time to breathe, time to appreciate what has come before, and time to prepare for what is to come (Mark 6:31; Matt. 11:28-29).

PART III

Retreats

His Eye Is on the Sparrow
God's Lace
Uniquely Wonderful

His Eye Is on the Sparrow

Options

One-Day Seminar
Women's Overnight Retreat   Women's Banquet

Decorations

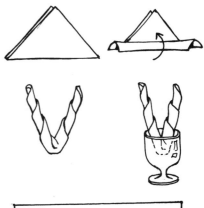

Tables   Cover with white tablecloths and use royal blue and bright gold napkins folded in a bird-wing design. Use alternate colors.

Centerpieces   One or a combination of these:

Potted trees   Dried branches, 8" to 10" tall (remove all leaves); set in small clay pots with plaster of paris. Attach tiny birds on all the branches. Trim rim of pot with blue ribbon and bow. Use Spanish moss (available at your local craft store) to cover the plaster and make a tiny nest, gluing it among the branches. Glue three tiny breath mints in the nest for eggs.

Sandwich board posters   (See Resources.)

Bird nests   Make your own nests with Spanish moss, available at your local craft store. Artificial eggs and a loose feather give the hint that a bird has just left.

Program Covers   (See Appendix, Item 3-A.)

Name Tags   Guests—On a 2½" x 4" card, using a blue stamp pad, place a blue thumbprint in one corner with a beak, tail, legs, and so on, added with marker to represent a bird. Print or do calligraphy of "His eye is on . . ." at the top, leaving room for the name.

Hostesses/Workers—Use owl pattern in Appendix, Item 3-B.

Wreaths   Obtain grapevine or straw wreaths from your local craft store and decorate with ribbon, flowers, a nest, some eggs, and a small artificial bird. Use as wall decorations and then as gifts for your speakers, pianist, and song leader.

Banner   Hand-letter or print on computer "His Eye Is on the Sparrow" and trim with blue and yellow ribbon. Hang above the speaker. The banner should be 8' to 10' long (or more, depending on the size of the platform area).

Posters   Draw on poster board:

1. A mother bird with her wings spread out wide and lots of little bird faces peering out from underneath. Letter it *"He shall cover thee with his feathers, and under his wings shalt thou trust (Ps. 91:4)."*

2. A little bird in the corner with one wing in a sling and a little tear sliding down one cheek. Letter it . . . *"One of them shall not fall on the ground without your Father (Matt. 10:29)."*

Special Features

Music

Background music   Taped bird-singing (See Resources.)

Theme song   "His Eye Is on the Sparrow" sung by soloist with pianist or taped accompaniment

The Story Behind the Hymn "His Eye Is on the Sparrow"   (See Resources.)

Visual Aids   One for each devotional topic (for each nest). (See Appendix, Items 3-C. 3-D, 3-E, 3-F, 3-G, and 3-H.) Enlarge and place on poster board to set on easel for speakers or devotions, or reduce and put inside the program.

Devotional

(See Resources.)

1. The Single Nest—singleness
2. The Love Nest—engagement or early marriage
3. The Full Nest—raising the family
4. Stricken Nest—tragedy befalls, i.e., the death of a spouse or child
5. The Empty Nest—children leave home
6. The Borrowed Nest—others living in your home temporarily or long-term

Food

Quiche or croissants with chicken salad

Melon balls in lettuce cup

Dinner rolls

Coffee or tea

Schedule Options

One-Day Seminar

9:00-9:30	Welcome, prayer, theme song, hymn story
9:30-10:00	Theme song, verse 1; Speaker 1 (Single Nest)
10:00-10:30	Theme song, refrain; Speaker 2 (Love Nest)
10:30-11:00	Coffee break
11:00-11:30	Reading: "Overheard in an Orchard" (see Resources); Speaker 3 (Full Nest)
11:30-1:00	Lunch
1:00-1:30	Theme song, verse 2; Speaker 4 (Stricken Nest)
1:30-2:00	Reading: letter from Joahna; Speaker 5 (Empty Nest)
2:00-2:30	Coffee break
2:30-3:00	Theme song, verse 3; Speaker 6 (Borrowed Nest)
3:00-3:45	Panel to address questions
3:45-4:00	Closing, dismissal—Wing Your Way Home.

Women's Overnight Retreat

Friday evening (may or may not schedule dinner)

6:00-7:00	Registration/get-acquainted time; hors d'oeuvres and punch (if not serving dinner)
7:00-7:30	Welcome, theme song, hymn story
7:30-8:15	Speaker—Stricken Nest

| 8:15-8:45 | Postsession (attend session of choice) |
| 8:45-9:00 | Overview of tomorrow's program; closing prayer |

Saturday

7:00-8:00	Breakfast and prepare for the day
8:00-8:30	Quiet time
8:30-9:45	Session 1 and postsession
9:45-10:15	Coffee break
10:15-11:30	Session 2 and postsession
11:30-12:00	Free time for fellowship
12:00-1:30	Lunch break
1:30-2:45	Session 3 and postsession
2:45-3:15	Coffee/soft drinks/juices
3:15-4:00	Panel of speakers—question and answer
	Say farewells and thank-yous;
	Take flight homeward.

Session Schedule:
Choose one lesson each session.

Session 1:	Single Nest
	Love Nest
	Borrowed Nest
Session 2:	Full Nest
	Love Nest
	Empty Nest
Session 3:	Full Nest
	Empty Nest
	Borrowed Nest

Postsession Suggestions:

Each postsession activity can be used as an open discussion with everyone participating or as a demonstration, such as food preparation. If available, a qualified professional could conduct a time for questions and answers, such as a counselor on grieving. Organizer should *choose one topic for each nest,* providing audience participation and varying each from session to session.

I. Single Nest
   A. Single and happy
      (How to be a happy single)
   B. Opportunities galore
      (Opportunities for service and self)
   C. Make me a blessing
      (What can I do for others?)

II. Love Nest
   A. How to have a vacation without going away
      (Ideas)
   B. Budget meals by candlelight
      (Preparing table and meals for two with recipes and tastes for all)
   C. Keep the love-lights burning
      (Ideas for keeping romance aflame)

III. Full Nest
   A. Better than mud pies
      (Kids' craft ideas or healthful snack ideas)
   B. Always room for one more

(Foster parenting, in-home day care, or loving your child's friends)

C. Don't forget the "worm digger"
(Ways to honor Dad and make him feel special)

IV. Stricken Nest
A. The sky is falling! The sky is falling!
(Prepare for tragedy through Scripture)
B. How to survive widowhood
(And how to help someone survive)
C. Understanding the grieving process
(Use qualified professional)

V. Empty Nest
A. Tea for two
(Enjoying each other, picnics, trips, fishing, crafts, and so on)
B. Filling empty days
(Jobs, activities, services, volunteer jobs)
C. The new challenge
(Caring for aging parents)

VI. Borrowed Nest
A. Hospitality can be fun
(Ideas for easily being hospitable)
B. A glass of iced tea in Jesus' name
(Little things mean so much)
C. Throw in another potato
(How to deal with unexpected guests)

RESOURCES

Sandwich Board Posters

(See Appendix, Item 3-I.) Sandwich boards are double-sided with a 2½" base. Use light cardboard and a color to fit your color scheme. They should be approximately 6" to 8" high.

Taped Bird-Singing

Most music stores dealing in compact discs, tapes, and records can order tapes of bird-singing from a number of sources.

The Story Behind the Hymn
"His Eye Is on the Sparrow"

Although Civilla D. Martin and Charles H. Gabriel had penned the words and written the music to "His Eye Is on the Sparrow" decades before, it is said that on a Sunday morning in the mid-1940s, a little sparrow flew into a Methodist church sanctuary in Virginia, disrupting the service. Eventually the bird landed on the organ pipes and kept an eagle eye on the congregation until the message was completed. As mysteriously as he had come, he flew away.

The incident reminded the minister of the story in Matt. 10:29: "Are not two sparrows sold for a farthing? And one of them shall not fall on the ground without your Father." In Luke 12:6, Jesus said again, "Are not five sparrows sold for two farthings, and not one of them is forgotten before God?"

Two sparrows sold for one penny, while, for two pennies, you not only got four sparrows but a fifth one thrown in for good measure. But even that poor, neglected, forgotten fifth sparrow was known to the Heavenly Father![1]

Hints for Speakers and Devotionals

1. Each speaker should take from 20 to 30 minutes (maximum) to cover each subject.
2. Place an easel next to each speaker with the enlarged drawing of the particular nest that speaker is representing. (See Appendix, Items 3-C, 3-D, 3-E, 3-F, 3-G, and 3-H.)
3. For the retreat schedule, each speaker is part of the panel that answers submitted questions.
4. Let participants break up for one discussion session on the nest of their choice. The discussion leaders should be the speakers from the various nests.

Devotional Ideas for Speakers

THE SINGLE NEST   Living a useful and happy life as a single person has real advantages and blessings. They may be used of God in ways others cannot, because often their time is more flexible and their family obligations not so overwhelming. You may want to give examples of these ways (i.e., volunteer work, baby-sitting, running errands for the elderly, etc.).

THE LOVE NEST   Remembering the sparkle and excitement of early marriage (as well as the importance of purity before marriage) can encourage us that it is never too late to spice things up. Maybe someone can share a few of their precious engagement and early-marriage memories (whether recent or in years past).

THE FULL NEST   "Digging worms," "cleaning the nest," and "giving flying lessons" every day keeps mothers busy with little time for anything else. Give some helpful hints for shopping, housekeeping, and occupying the children.

THE STRICKEN NEST   Coping with grief, anger, fear, bitterness, or loneliness is often a task we didn't plan for in life. Helping our children cope is very important. Give suggestions for what a church can do to lend a hand at these times. Perhaps present the importance of building a strong relationship with the God of all comfort.
   "If thou faint in the day of adversity, thy strength is small" (Prov. 24:10).

THE EMPTY NEST   Challenging those who feel lonely and left with nothing to do when those fledglings fly the coop is very important. An empty nest is still functional and can be enjoyable. Tell how to prepare yourself and your children for the emptying of the nest by giving suggestions of what to look forward to (time with your spouse, freedom to travel, etc.) and how you can spend time on things you may have been putting off for years (reading special books, cleaning a forgotten closet, baking cookies for grandkids, etc.).

---

1. Adapted from Ernest K. Emurian, *Forty Stories of Famous Gospel Songs* (Grand Rapids: Baker Book House, 1984), 44-47.

THE BORROWED NEST   Opening our home for others is sometimes what the Lord would like us to do. Jesus' friends opened their homes to Him, giving us the example of hospitality. Encourage everyone to find appropriate times to "open their nests" to visitors, whether short-term or long-term. Remember that receiving hospitality is often as important as being hospitable.

Is It Really Worth It?

by Nora Burdett

The strange old woman walked into the beautifully decorated banquet hall. She looked (and smelled) conspicuously out of place. Every guest had been seated and served a delicious meal. The old woman was unsure of what she should do next.

No, she didn't have a ticket or a friend, and she was more alone than any of us knew. We made room for her at our table and tried to help her with her bag and coat. She clung to them ferociously. We served her a meal and tried to make conversation. Her eyes darted about the table like wild fawns startled by hunters. She ate so fast we feared she would choke.

I hope we didn't stare. (I *know* we did!) I trust we seemed more relaxed in her presence than she was in ours. (I'm *sure* we weren't!) I hope we made her feel welcome, comfortable, and loved—we tried!

She was a bagwoman. Everything she owned she either carried in her large bag or wore. She had been a woman of some means long ago, but life had dealt her one too many blows. She lived on the streets, out of trash cans, and slept wherever she could.

She noticed that something was on at church as she walked by and in desperation decided to see if they might be offering any food. Indeed, she was fed—both body and soul. Temporary accommodations for the night were arranged, and the next day they found something more permanent. But most important, that night she met our friend, our Lord and Savior, Jesus Christ.

This did not happen in some poor ghetto of a large city—but rather in an exceptionally affluent suburb of southern California. I remember and commend those ladies for their unselfish love and concern for that poor woman. Through a banquet, and all the work and fun that entailed for them, they were able to reach out to a needy, hurting individual in a way she will never forget. Maybe they knew the secret of Heb. 13:2— "Be not forgetful to entertain strangers; for thereby some have entertained angels unawares."

Overheard in an Orchard

by Elizabeth Cheney

Said the Robin to the Sparrow:
"I should really like to know
Why these anxious human beings
Rush about and worry so."

Said the Sparrow to the Robin:
"Friend, I think that it must be
That they have no heavenly Father,
Such as cares for you and me."

Empty-Nest Reading

This letter was received from Joahna Keller Koning, daughter of Karen Keller.

Dear Mom,

I thought of an event that illustrates the empty-nest syndrome from my perspective in a particularly poignant way.

One spring a pair of barn swallows built a nest on Mrs. Jones's porch. We enjoyed watching them bring in just the right combination of twigs and hay. We circled our chairs around the living room window so that we could watch the construction each day.

We watched as the mother laid her eggs and as the papa swallow took his turn sitting on the nest. We watched as the mother and father swooped down on the wild cats that tried to climb the pillar. We watched as they weathered spring storms and several frosty nights. And finally the precious eggs hatched.

Over the next two weeks the proud couple fed and cared for their new brood. They brought worms and bits and pieces of food to eat, and they taught them all the inner workings of a nest. Eventually they taught the babies to fly.

One day, as nature dictates, the baby birds flew away. The mother and the father hung around for a few days and then abandoned the nest to go on with their lives.

Several days later Mrs. Jones, Liza, and I were sitting out on the porch—safe once again from the angry, swooping father so anxious to protect his young. We were startled to see a baby swallow fly back to the now-abandoned nest. He sat for a moment on the edge of the nest and chirped out in a most frantic manner. Nobody came. He jumped into the nest and continued to call out—but nobody came. The nest was truly empty.

He chirped and cried for the better part of two days. His pitiful song could be heard day and night. After two days we woke to a quiet dawn, and I thought the bird had finally flown away to start his own life.

Several days later, Liza and I complied with Mrs. Jones's request to get rid of the nest. We climbed up on a step-ladder and proceeded to dismantle the art of nature. I wanted to try and remove the nest intact, so we carefully picked away the mud and twigs around the main nest until we could take it down.

As we got the nest to eye level, we were saddened to see the baby barn swallow lying dead in the bowl of the nest. The poor little bird had needed some extra time, attention, love, or maybe just a warm place to rest while someone fed him and cared for his needs. So he returned home, but his home was now just an empty nest.

Our nest is not empty. You and Daddy still roost there together. You are always there for us should we need to fly home for comfort, protection, or just a rest. Perhaps it seems a bit lonely for you at times; perhaps it is too quiet. But you are maintaining the nest for all of us. You have never abandoned the nest. There is no greater comfort to me than to know that if I need you, you are there. Our nest is full, our nest is intact, our nest is like a security blanket that wraps me and shelters me every day. Because you taught us how to build nests and how to live life successfully, when the time comes and you need a nest to rest in, somewhere to go to be cared for and loved, you will have two full nests to choose from. So our nest is not empty—our nest is very full.

Love,
Joahna

GOD'S LACE

Option

Women's Overnight Retreat

Decorations

Tables   Use solid navy, black, or royal blue tablecloths under white or cream lace tablecloths.

Centerpieces   White doily luminarias. (See Resources.)

Program Cover   (See Appendix, Item 3-J: Options A and B.)

Name Tags   Glue a strip of lace across the top of pastel-colored 2¼" x 4" cards. Write names by hand.

Banner   "In quietness and in confidence shall be your strength (Isa. 30:15)." Banner should be 8' to 10' long (or more, depending on the size of the platform area).

Special Features

Get-Acquainted Game   (See Resources.)

Food

Snacks and Meals   (See Resources.)

*   *   *

Introductory Remarks

This is a unique retreat. Lace is created by forming delicate patterns when the fibers are purposely left open at intervals, thus creating spaces. Much work is required to create the intricate designs, but it is the open spaces that make us appreciate that workmanship. Our lives are made more valuable and beautiful as we weave in open spaces. We can create space in our lives. Other spaces God creates for us.

This weekend will be different. It is not a time for frivolity. We are going to see how to find the "quietness and confidence" for our lives through solitude, meditation, and yieldedness. We are going to ask you to do some things that are somewhat different. If you can cooperate, you will be blessed.

1. Please "forget" to wear your watches tomorrow.
2. Concentrate on what God wants to do in you.
3. Keep a pen and pad handy to jot down thoughts you'd like to share later.

SUGGESTED SCHEDULE FOR RETREAT

Friday Evening

7:00-7:30   Welcome/Get-acquainted game
            Introduction to theme

7:30-9:00   Hymn—*Have Thine Own Way*
            Speaker—*God's Lace*
            Give an introduction to lace—such as history, purpose, examples (could use an overhead showing various lace

samples). Emphasize salvation (for the lost) and self-examination (for the saved), for without the hand of the Master Craftsman working in us, we can never become God's lace masterpiece.

1. There is a master craftsman for each piece.
2. There is a plan for every piece of lace.

Following the evening service, have a time of individual, silent prayer. As each person is finished, she may quietly leave the building. Have personal workers available. Light refreshments may be served in another room (see Resources).

Saturday
8:00-9:00   Breakfast (See Resources.)
9:00-9:45   Speaker
            Solitude

1. It is something *we* choose to do.
2. It is more a state of mind than a place.
3. It is different from loneliness.
4. You need a quiet place to practice it.
5. It was practiced by Christ.
6. It is a scriptural thing to do: Matt. 4:11; Luke 6:12; Mark 6:31; Matt. 14:23; 26:36-46.
7. The fruit of it is sensitivity and compassion for others.

Encourage guests to experience this morning's subjects by observing total silence *from now until after lunch.*

9:45-10:30   Practice solitude
            Spend time experiencing the presence of God. Enjoy the silence. Enjoy His handiwork—His light, His air, His creation. Observe lace patterns in nature, such as lacy fernleaf, decayed leaf, and the lacy pattern of tree against sky.
10:30-10:45   Break
            Have midmorning snacks (see Resources) for ladies to enjoy while they listen to the next speaker.
10:45-11:30   Speaker
            Meditation

1. It is something *we* choose to do.
2. It is a scriptural thing to do: Gen. 24:63; Pss. 63:6; 119:148; 1:2.
3. There is a difference between Eastern meditation and Christian meditation.
   a. Eastern meditation is an attempt to *empty* the mind.
   b. Christian meditation is an attempt to *fill* the mind —with the things of God.
4. It gives birth to praise.
5. It gives us the ability to hear God's voice and obey His Word.
6. It creates inner space for God to meet with us.
7. There are three kinds of meditation:
   a. *meditation on a specific scripture,* such as John 14:27. Memorizing Scripture makes it easier for us to meditate on it more frequently.
   b. *recollection or "palms down, palms up" method*

> (1) palms down—turning our concerns over to God
>
> (2) palms up—accepting God's provision for each concern
>
> c. *meditation on God's creation,* as in Ps. 19:1

11:30-12:15   Practice Meditation
1. Try one of the above methods of meditation.
2. Write down anything special God reveals to you during this time.

12:15-1:00   Lunch (See Resources.)

Play soft music to prevent some from feeling uneasy during the quietness.

1:00-2:00   Speaker

Yieldedness

1. Sometimes *God* chooses space for us, such as in illness, loss, or waiting.
2. It can be God's way of weaving into our lives open space that we would not choose ourselves.
3. He does all things well.
4. We must simply yield ourselves to His care and control at these times, thanking Him for the space and for what He plans to do through it.
5. Review these scriptures: Psalm 37; Prov. 3:5-6; 2 Corinthians 1; Isa. 30:15.

2:00-3:00   Discussion

Lead the group in a very short overview of each message and its relationship to the aim of the retreat. Open for discussion and questions. Perhaps use your speakers to form a panel to help keep discussion rolling and on target, but allow guests to do the majority of the talking and sharing—they will be the best gauge to test your teaching.

3:00-4:00   Afternoon Tea

Plan a very special, very fancy afternoon tea with lace tablecloths, silver tea and coffee service, a deliciously elegant snack, and anything that would enhance the theme and send the guests home on a nice note.

RESOURCES

Centerpieces

Use lunch-size white or brown paper bags and small paper doilies. Cut out a portion of each side of the bag slightly smaller than the size of the doily. Around the edge of each doily use a glue stick; then place over cutout on bag. Fold down the top edge of the bag approximately 1½". In the bottom of the bag place a votive candleholder with lighted candle.

Get-Acquainted Game

Prepare half as many pieces of various sizes, colors, and types of lace (available at your local fabric store) as the number of guests (100 guests: 50 pieces of lace). Cut each piece in half and give one-half to each guest as she arrives. The object is to find the person with the other half of the lace that matches and sit with that person for a few minutes.

Each group of two should find out two things: one thing they have in common and one thing they each know about lace.

Snacks and Meals

Friday Night Snacks: Serve popcorn and hot apple cider; or cookies, coffee, tea, and hot chocolate. Remember to have plenty of decaffeinated drinks available.

Saturday Breakfast: Banana-Orange Slush*
Mini Breakfast Quiches*
Broiled Peach Halves*

Saturday Midmorning Snack: Healthful Bran Muffins*
Banana-Orange Slush*
Coffee, tea, milk

Saturday Lunch: Sandwich and Salad Smorgasbord
Trays of meats and cheeses; baskets of breads; lettuce and tomato slices; condiments
Fresh salads, including fruit salad
Iced tea, coffee

Saturday Afternoon Tea: Peach Punch*
Petits fours on silver trays
Fancy layer cakes on cake stands
Cookies, bars, candies
Fresh strawberries half dipped in white or milk chocolate
Cheese and crackers
Refrigerator Lace Cookies*
Coffee and tea served in silver
Confetti or sparkles all over tablecloth

Recipes

Banana-Orange Slush

1 cup sugar
2 cups boiling water
1 6-ounce can frozen orange juice concentrate, undiluted
1 15-ounce can crushed pineapple
1 10-ounce jar maraschino cherries, drained
3 bananas, peeled and sliced
2½ tablespoons lemon juice
Fresh mint sprigs (optional)

Combine all ingredients except mint; mix well. Freeze overnight or until firm. Remove from freezer 15 to 20 minutes before serving (mixture

*Recipes following.

99

should be slushy when served). Garnish with fresh mint sprigs if desired. Yield: about 2 quarts.

Mini Breakfast Quiches

1 pound freshly cooked broccoli (chopped fine)
24 slices whole wheat bread (crusts trimmed)
2¼ cups shredded cheddar cheese
1 cup finely chopped ham
5 eggs
2 tablespoons minced onion
1¾ cup milk
2 teaspoons dry mustard
2 teaspoons Worcestershire sauce
½ teaspoon salt
½ teaspoon garlic powder
Dash cayenne

Trim crusts from bread. Lightly spray muffin pans with nonstick spray. Fit one slice of bread into each muffin cup. Sprinkle cheese evenly over the bottom of all 24 muffin cups. Top with ham and broccoli until evenly distributed.

In bowl, beat eggs. Add onion, mustard, Worcestershire sauce, salt, garlic, and cayenne. Add milk and blend well. Pour evenly over layered ingredients. Cover and refrigerate for at least 8 hours or overnight. Bake uncovered, 350° F. for 15 minutes. Top with remaining cheese and bake additional 5 minutes or until items appear firm. Serve immediately.

Broiled Peach Halves

Drain 12 canned peach halves and pat dry with paper towel. Place cut side up on nonstick cookie sheet. Lightly drizzle ½ cup whipping cream over peaches. Sprinkle with brown sugar and a little cinnamon. Place under broiler until sugar bubbles. Serve warm.

Healthful Bran Muffins

1 15-ounce package wheat bran flakes with raisins
5 cups all-purpose flour
3 cups sugar
1 tablespoon plus 2 teaspoons soda
2 teaspoons salt
4 eggs, beaten
4 cups buttermilk
1 cup vegetable oil

Combine first 5 ingredients in large bowl. Make a well in center of mixture. Add eggs, buttermilk, and oil; stir just enough to moisten dry ingredients. Cover and store in refrigerator until ready to bake. (Batter can be stored in refrigerator up to 6 weeks.)

When ready to bake, fill greased muffin pans two-thirds full. Bake at 400° F. for 12 to 15 minutes.

Yield: about 5½ dozen.

Peach Punch

2 cups sugar
1 cup water
1 3-ounce package peach gelatin
2 cups hot water
1 16-ounce can frozen lemonade

4 lemonade cans water
1 46-ounce can pineapple juice
1 46-ounce can peach drink
1 quart peach soda

Mix sugar and 1 cup water together and boil for a few minutes. Dissolve gelatin in 2 cups water. Add to sugar gelatin mixture. Add lemonade, water, pineapple juice, and peach drink. Mix well. Put into large containers and freeze for about 12 hours. Set out to thaw about 6 hours before use. Stir before serving (should be slushy). Add peach soda just before serving. Makes 6 quarts or 35 servings.

Note: Make an ice ring from the punch mixture instead of water to keep from diluting punch. Just pour punch mixture (before adding peach soda) into a ring mold or bundt cake pan. Freeze solid. (Frozen peach soda can be used for the ring as well.)

Refrigerator Lace Cookies

Stir until well blended:
½ cup white sugar
½ cup brown sugar
¾ cup sifted all-purpose flour
½ teaspoon each soda and salt
½ cup soft butter
1 egg
1 tablespoon milk
1½ teaspoon grated orange or lemon rind
½ teaspoon almond or vanilla extract

Work in with hands:
1 cup rolled oats

After mixing dough, form it into a 2" diameter roll on a piece of foil, in which you wrap it securely. Chill the roll for 12 to 24 hours, after which it can be very thinly sliced for baking—the thinner the lacier.

Bake on a greased cookie sheet in a 400° F. oven for 8 to 10 minutes. Refrigerator cookies freeze well, baked or unbaked.

Yield: about 60 (2") cookies.

UNIQUELY WONDERFUL

Options

Women's Meeting   One-Day Retreat   Teen Retreat
Children's Meeting

Decorations

Program Covers   (See Appendix, Item 3-K.)

Name Tags   On a 2½" x 4" card, using a stamp pad, place a thumbprint near the left-hand edge and add arms, legs, and so on. Print or do calligraphy of the word "Uniquely," with a line beneath for the individual's name.

Special Features

Game   (See Resources.)

Visuals for Devotional   Small, differently wrapped packages (See Resources.)

Devotional

Woven into the opening of the packages (See Resources.)

Food

Devonshire tea

Savory chicken parcels

Special garden salad

Fruit kabobs with coconut dressing
(See Resources.)

One-Day Retreat Schedule

(Intersperse the reading of the personality cards. See Resources—Games.)

9:00-10:00   Devotional
10:00-10:30   Break (serve Devonshire tea)
10:30-11:15   Speaker and workshop—temperaments (See Resources.)
11:15-12:00   Speaker and workshop—spiritual gifts (See Resources.)
12:00-1:00   Lunch
1:00-1:30   Study time to assimilate and personally apply previous lessons
1:30-2:30   Speaker—areas of service (See Resources.)
2:30-3:30   Discussion Time

RESOURCES

Game

As guests arrive, have them fill out a small "personality" card, answering these questions about themselves:

1. How tall are you?
2. What is your favorite hobby?
3. If you had one entire week to do as you pleased without any concern for money or typical time limitations, what would you do?
4. What is your most dreaded household chore?
5. If you could go alone to any car lot you wished and select whatever automobile you wanted with no worries about the price tag, what would you choose?

Have them deposit the cards in a box, where they will be drawn out randomly during the retreat and read to the audience.

Visuals for Devotional

Some suggestions of the contents of wrapped packages and their interpretations:

1. *Pencil*—one who is useful but may need sharpening.
2. *Used tea bag*—one who has nothing fresh to give.
3. *Candy bar*—one who is sweet but not that good for you.
4. *Potato peeler*—one who is sharp, useful, and trained.
5. *Empty box*—one who has no spiritual depth, no active relationship with Christ, and no ability to share anything.
6. *Craft kit*—one who is launching into something new.
7. *Seconds or damaged goods*—one who is missing the mark.
8. *Needle*—one who is sharp, with a single eye (single-minded), and useful.
9. *Eraser*—one who rights wrongs; one who can say, "I was wrong," or "I am sorry."
10. *White flag*—one who is surrendered to God, or a peacemaker.
11. *Cookie mix*—one who is at his or her best when the heat is on.

Devotional

Encourage everyone to choose a package. Show the packages and talk about each one. Ask people, "Why did you choose your gift?" Some will say they chose it because it was big, pretty, plain, fancy, interesting-looking, and so on.

Have each person with a package open it. Lead a discussion about the significance of each item, using audience participation as much as possible in relating the items to personality types.

Each person present is unique. Some are prettier on the outside than others. Some have larger frames than others. Some are dressed better than others. Some look really dressy, others more casual. While it does matter how we take care of the outside of our lives, what really matters is the inside. We can be filled and useful on the inside—or empty and useless. Expound for a while on the scripture 1 Sam. 16:7: "for the Lord seeth not as man seeth; for man looketh on the outward appearance, but the Lord looketh on the heart."

Human beings are prone to be drawn to the most attractive people, the most popular, the wealthiest, the funniest, or the smartest. Rarely do people seek out unattractive, unpopular, poor, dull, or dismal people. If we would just take the time to get to know them, we would find that many times the plain, quiet people are those of depth with wisdom to share. But "man looketh on the outward appearance."

Everyone has a heart with what could be described as a "God-shaped vacuum." Only God can make our lives what they truly ought to be. He awaits our invitation for Him to come in and do that work and fill that void. Regardless of what we look like on the outside, we should always strive to look our best. God sees us on the inside and knows what we are really like. "But the Lord looketh on the heart."

Perhaps we are like some of the packages that have just been opened. Some look prettier, cleaner, neater on the outside than others. Some people are outwardly more popular, smarter, wittier, or more fun than others. But what is on the inside? There may be bad character, negative attitudes, or just emptiness. Jesus is able to replace the old man with the new. He may not change the color of our hair, the shape of our face, the size of our ears, or the curve of our nose, but when we really have something worthwhile inside from God, people will learn to appreciate those things, and the outside will become secondary.

We are uniquely wonderful! We are "fearfully and wonderfully made" (Ps. 139:14). While we must make the best of the outward appearance, we must also be sure to take more time for the inside. We must be sure we have accepted Jesus Christ as our personal Savior and Lord. We need to grow in Him daily as we read our Bibles, pray, and surrender our wills to His.

When choosing friends, we should look for good inner qualities in them. We should choose our close friends from those who encourage us with positive attitudes and strive to help the ones who have trouble in those areas. We need to be wise about becoming involved with people who pull us down or try to tempt us to do things that aren't right, even though these people may seem great on the outside. Look for ways of loving them to the Lord. Let us look for the best in people but beware of the worst. Be discerning! Finally, we should ask ourselves, "What kind of package am I?"

Temperaments

We have each inherited a basic temperament from our parents. This temperament gives us our qualities of uniqueness and individuality. Temperament is the combined traits we receive genetically. Character is the real you. Personality is how we express ourselves to others. Four basic temperament types were recognized long ago by Hippocrates and later developed by modern writers.

1. Sanguine—extrovert type.

STRENGTHS	WEAKNESSES
Enjoys life	Restless
Optimistic	Weak-willed
Friendly	Egotistical
Compassionate	Emotionally unstable

2. Choleric—extrovert type.

STRENGTHS	WEAKNESSES
Strong-willed	Hot-tempered
Practical	Cruel
Leader	Impetuous
Optimistic	Self-sufficient

3. Melancholy—introvert type.

STRENGTHS	WEAKNESSES
Sensitive	Self-centered
Perfectionist	Pessimistic
Faithful friend	Moody
Self-sacrificing	Revengeful

4. Phlegmatic—introvert type.

STRENGTHS	WEAKNESSES
Witty	Slow and lazy
Dependable	Tease
Efficient	Selfish and stubborn
	Indecisive[1]

The Christian, through the power of the Holy Spirit, has the fruit of the Spirit, which is love, joy, peace, longsuffering, gentleness, goodness, faith, meekness, and temperance (Gal. 5:22-23). By using these tools, a Christian can overcome the weaknesses and improve the strengths of each temperament:

1. Face your weaknesses and any
   unconfessed sin.   Prov. 28:13
2. Confess and forsake your sin.   1 John 1:9
3. Believe God has given the victory.   1 Cor. 15:57
4. Ask for the refilling of the Holy Spirit. Luke 11:13
5. Walk in the Spirit and abide in Christ.   Gal. 5:16; John 15:7

Temperament tests are available in many books on this study and could be given. They are available at Christian bookstores.

Spiritual Gifts

When we accept Christ, we are given spiritual gifts. Everyone has at least one. Your natural talent may be a key. Rom. 12:3-8 lists the gifts:

1. PROPHECY   Rom. 12:6; 1 Cor. 14:3—to desire to reveal wrong motives and actions by presenting the truth. Example of Jesus rebuking the money changers: Mark 11:15-17.

2. SERVING   Rom. 12:7—understands and meets the needs of the practical side of life. Example of Jesus washing the feet of His disciples: John 13:1-17

3. TEACHING   Rom. 12:7; 2 Tim. 2:1-2—the ability to clarify the truths of God's Word through research and instruction. Example of Jesus rejecting men's traditions of Scripture and teaching true principles: Matt. 15:1-20.

4. EXHORTATION OR ENCOURAGING   Rom. 12:8—the ability to visualize specific achievements and prescribe precise steps of action. Example of Jesus with the rich young ruler: Matt. 19:16-26.

5. GIVING   Rom. 12:8, 13, 20—the ability to share oneself and material resources to meet specific needs. Example of Jesus laying down His life for His disciples and giving himself as a ransom for many: John 10:17-18; Matt. 20:28.

---

1. Adapted from *Spirit-controlled Temperament*, by Tim LaHaye, 211-19 © 1966 by Post, Inc., LaMesa, Calif. Revised edition © 1992 Tim LaHaye. Used by permission of Tyndale House Publishers, Inc. All rights reserved.

6. RULING   Rom. 12:8; 1 Tim. 3:4, 12—the ability to see the overall picture and inspire others to fulfill long-range goals. Example of Jesus calling His disciples to follow Him so that they could become fishers of men: Matt. 4:19.

7. MERCY   Rom. 12:8—The ability to empathize with the weaknesses of others and help them experience God's grace in time of need. Example of Jesus showing mercy, love, and compassion for the woman caught in adultery without condemning her: John 8:1-11.

It would seem from Scripture that we each have one main spiritual gift. Ask the Lord to help you discern your main gift and through His power develop it. There are many tests to help you determine what your main gift is.[2]

Areas of Service

Taking into consideration the following, you can better decide the area of service in which you can meaningfully make your contribution in the church. The pastor, minister of education, or other members of the church staff can help you find your specific place to serve.

1. Your temperament type
2. Your spiritual gift
3. Your natural talents
4. Your maturity in the Lord
5. Your availability for service
6. Your area of greatest concern (children, adults, outreach, etc.)

There are many varieties of service available in a church:

Teaching—different age-groups
Counseling—through discipleship, at the altar, over the telephone
Leadership areas
Encouragement
Evangelism
Hospitality—guests, entertaining visitors
Helping in a specific area

Devonshire Tea

Originates from Devon in England and consists of light little scones (American biscuits). Usually two whole scones are served per person. In small dishes, serve separately strawberry jam and whipped cream (use real whipped cream for best results). Break or cut the scone in half, and put on each half a teaspoon of jam followed by a dollop of cream. Serve with cups of hot coffee or tea, cream, and sugar.

Savory Chicken Parcels

3 ounces cream cheese, softened	2 tablespoons milk
3 tablespoons butter, melted	1 tablespoon chopped onion
2 cups cooked cubed chicken	1 tablespoon chopped pimento
¼ teaspoon salt	8-ounce can crescent rolls
⅛ teaspoon pepper	¾ cup seasoned croutons, crushed

---

2. Billy Hamm, *Discovering Your Spiritual Gift* (Denver: Mountain States Baptist Church, 1978), n.p. Used by permission.

Preheat oven to 350° F. In medium bowl, blend cream cheese and 2 tablespoons butter (reserve 1 tablespoon) until smooth. Add chicken, salt, pepper, milk, onion, and pimento. Mix well. Separate crescent dough into 4 rectangles. Firmly press perforations to seal. Spoon ½ cup meat mixture onto each rectangle. Pull 4 corners to top of center of meat mixture, twist slightly, and seal edges. Brush tops with reserved 1 tablespoon butter and sprinkle with crouton crumbs. Bake on ungreased cookie sheet for 20 to 25 minutes until golden brown.

Yield: 4.

Special Garden Salad

Broccoli, cut up   Cauliflowerets
Grated cheddar cheese   Ranch dressing
Bacon bits

Combine all ingredients in your chosen amounts. Chill 2 to 3 hours.

Fruit Kabobs with Coconut Dressing

Red apples   Seedless grapes, red or green
Pears   Fresh strawberries
Lemon juice   Coconut dressing
Unsweetened pineapple chunks

Cut apples and pears into bite-sized pieces. Add lemon juice; toss gently. Alternate apple, pineapple, grape, pear, and strawberry on a bamboo skewer. Repeat with remaining fruit. Serve with coconut dressing.

Coconut Dressing: 1½ cups vanilla low-fat yogurt
                     1½ tablespoon flaked coconut
                     1½ tablespoon reduced-calorie orange marmalade

Combine all ingredients and serve in small nut cups with each kabob.

Yield: 1⅔ cups.

APPENDIX

SCHEDULE FOR PLANNING A BANQUET OR PARTY

Three Months Before
1. Pray.
2. Choose theme and date.
3. Set budget.
4. Choose speaker and issue invitation.
5. Choose and secure location.
6. Organize function committees and plan details
   a. decorations and colors
   b. special features (skits, songs, readings, plays, poems, puppets, games, crafts, demonstrations)
   c. food (If using caterers, see when they need the final number of guests. Set menu. Do they provide table coverings and setups?) Will you have waiters and/or waitresses or serve buffet style?
   d. baby-sitters (You may need to be willing to pay for this service or exchange services with members of another local church.)
   e. fees, gifts, acknowledgments (for speaker, soloists or other guest performers, committee chairmen, etc.)
   f. publicity (posters, church bulletin, newpapers, local businesses, etc.)
   g. sound (public-address system, various microphones, and taping)
   h. cleanup

One Month Before
1. Reconfirm location reservations.
2. Encourage and remind speaker. See if he or she has any special needs or requirements. Make arrangements for his or her transportation and/or accommodations.
3. Check on committee leaders.
4. Set date for ticket sales (approximately 2 weeks before event).
5. Don't forget to pray!

One Week Before
1. Have daily prayer times.
2. Check with all committee members about their assignments.
3. Give caterers your final numbers.
4. Reconfirm all arrangements with speaker.
5. Decide what day you will decorate.

On the Day
1. Leaders and committee members arrive early.
2. Attend to last-minute decorations (set out flowers and so on).
3. Check sound system and recording equipment.
4. Set out glass of water for speaker.
5. Be sure honorarium is prepared for speaker and is in proper hands.
6. Go over order of events to make sure everything runs smoothly.
7. Relax before arrival of guests.

SCHEDULE FOR PLANNING A RETREAT

Six Months Before

1. Pray.
2. Choose theme and date.
3. Set budget.
4. Choose speaker and issue invitation.
5. Choose and secure location.
6. Plan details.
   - *a.* decorations and colors
   - *b.* special features
   - *c.* devotions
   - *d.* food
   - *e.* baby-sitters
   - *f.* fees

Two Months Before

1. Reconfirm location reservations.
2. Encourage and remind speaker.
3. Organize function committees (have a leader in each section).
   - *a.* decorations
   - *b.* special features
   - *c.* food
   - *d.* registration
   - *e.* cleanup
   - *f.* baby-sitters

One Month Before

1. Have prayer times.
2. Increase publicity, begin to sell tickets, and make reservations (nonrefundable).
3. Meet with committee leaders.

One Week Before

1. Check with each committee member.
2. Order flowers or fruit basket for speaker's room.
3. Finalize attendance numbers with caterers and retreat facility.

On the Day

1. Leaders and committee members arrive early.
2. Attend to last-minute decorations (set out flowers and so on).
3. Check sound system and recording equipment.
4. Set out glass of water for speaker.
5. Be sure honorarium is prepared for speaker and is in proper hands.
6. Go over order of events to make sure everything runs smoothly.
7. Relax before arrival of guests.

Patchwork Christmas

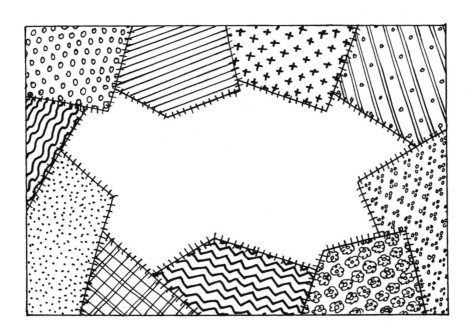

Item 1-C

Item 1-D

A Victorian Christmas

Item 1-F

Item 1-G

Item 1-J

Item 1-K

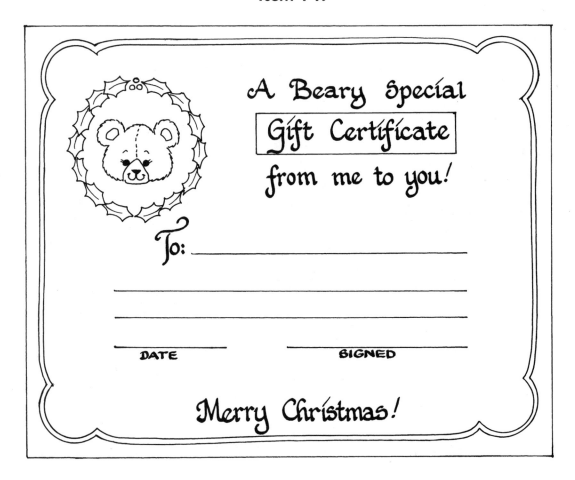

Dear Friend,

This little Bear Bag is especially for you with some ideas to help you get through the holiday hustle and bustle.
Remember the three special things that will help:
"Give to others"
"Make homespun fun"
"Make Christ the center of your Christmas"

Now—about the Bear Bag—you will find a "ginger" bear. He's carrying the ginger spice for your cookies.
Look a little further for a "cinnamon" bear to satisfy your sweet tooth.
The other bears will tell their own stories!

Your beary good friend,
"The Christmas Bear"

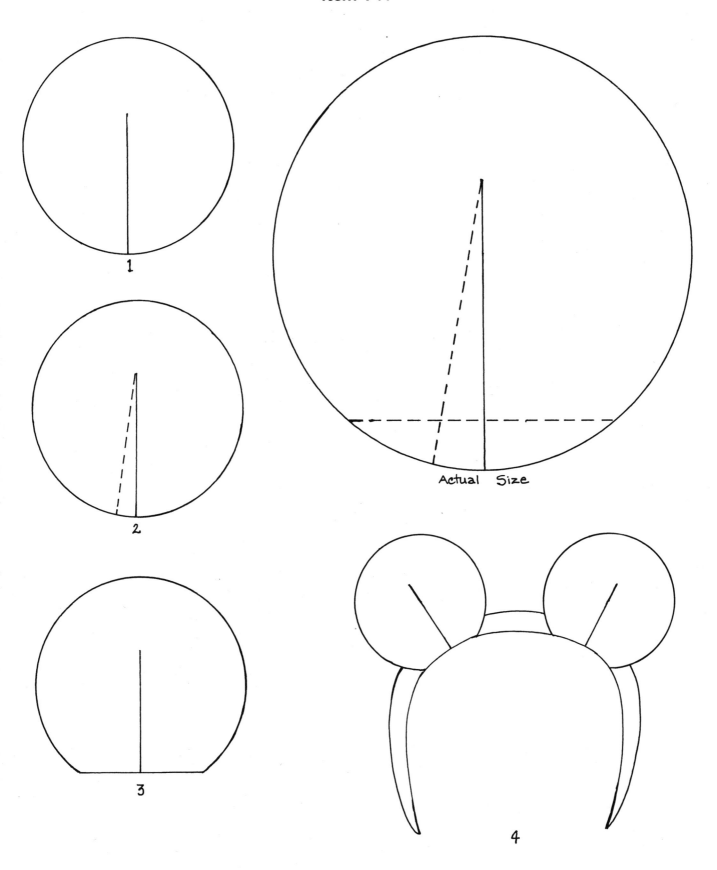

1

2

Actual Size

3

4

Item 1-O

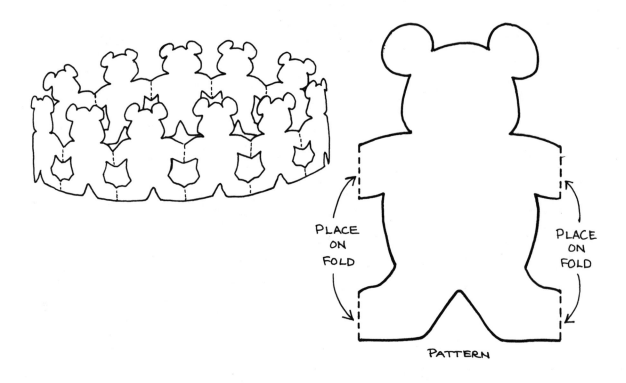

PLACE ON FOLD

PLACE ON FOLD

PATTERN

Item 1-P

Item 2-E

Fan Stands

These are made of cardboard in colors that go with the theme. Cut and fold. The words will be on the back side. Use several in groups turned at different angles so that they can be enjoyed from both sides of the table. Arrange silk flowers around and among the fans, creating a centerpiece effect on the tables.

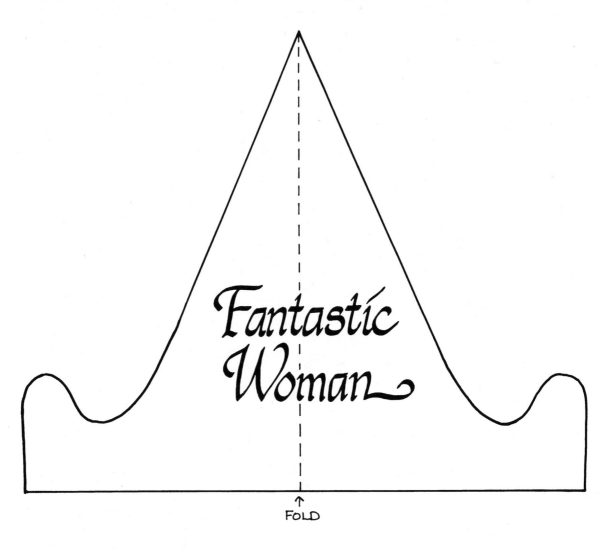

Fantastic Woman

↑
FOLD

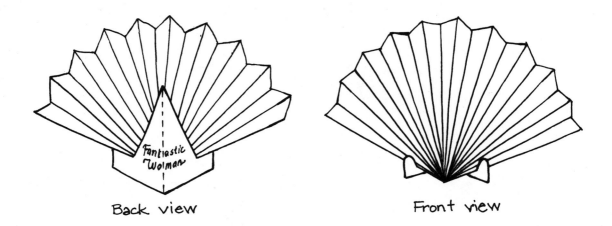

Back view   Front view

Fantastic
Woman

Item 2-G

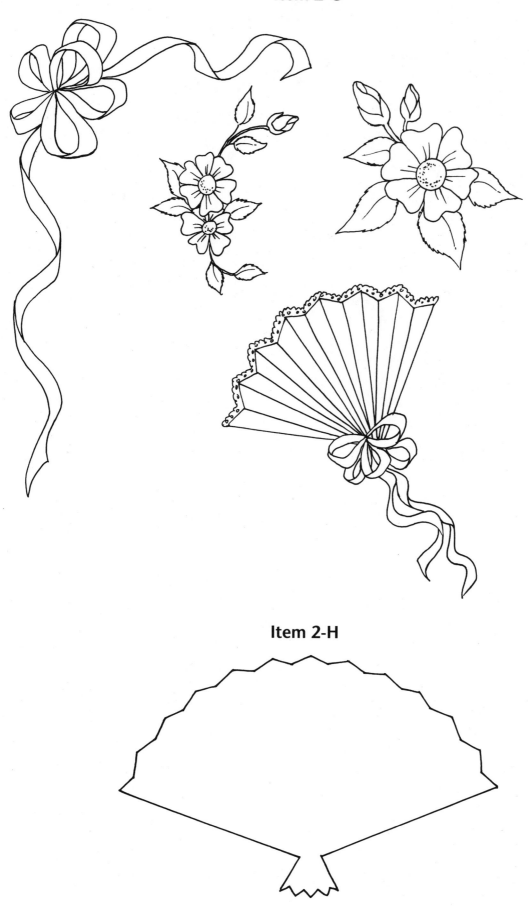

Item 2-H

Item 2-L

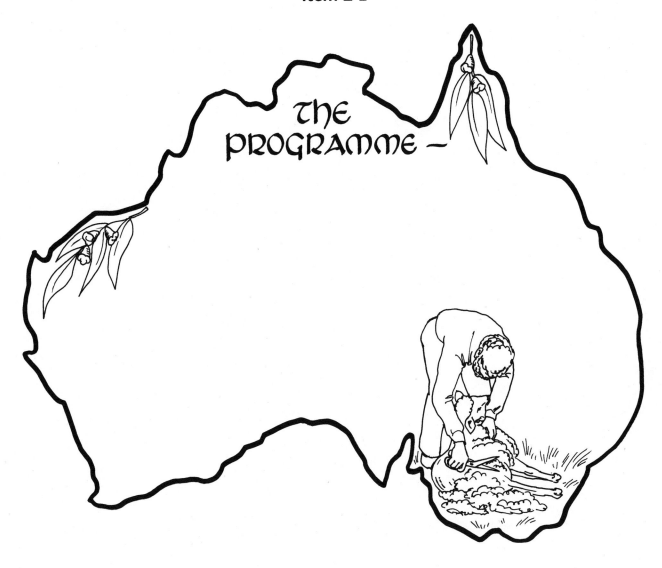

THE PROGRAMME —

Item 2-M

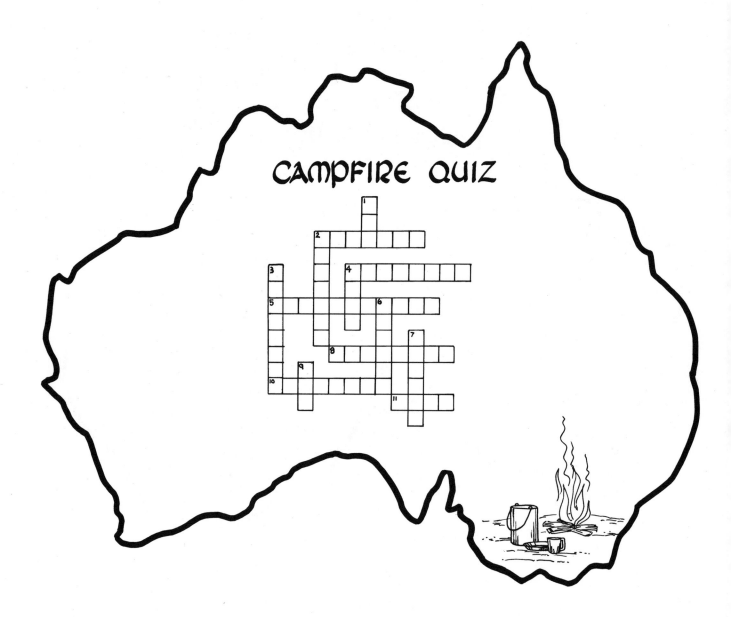

ACROSS

2. The _____ wanders the country with his swag on his back.
4. Large country properties are known as sheep and cattle _____ .
5. The men who drove cattle or sheep over long distances.
8. The outback men gather around the _____ at night to cook their meal.
10. The owner of the station property.
11. The food given to station workers for their weekly ration was usually flour, sugar, tea, and _____ .

DOWN

1. This animal helps his master control both sheep and cattle.
2. He cuts the fleece from the sheep.
3. The first settlers to live in an area are called its _____ .
4. The belongings and blanket of this man are rolled into a _____ .
6. The outback men cook and eat this instead of bread.
7. The _____ is the fastest shearer in the shearing shed.
9. The pioneers' first home in the bush was generally a rough, one-roomed _____.

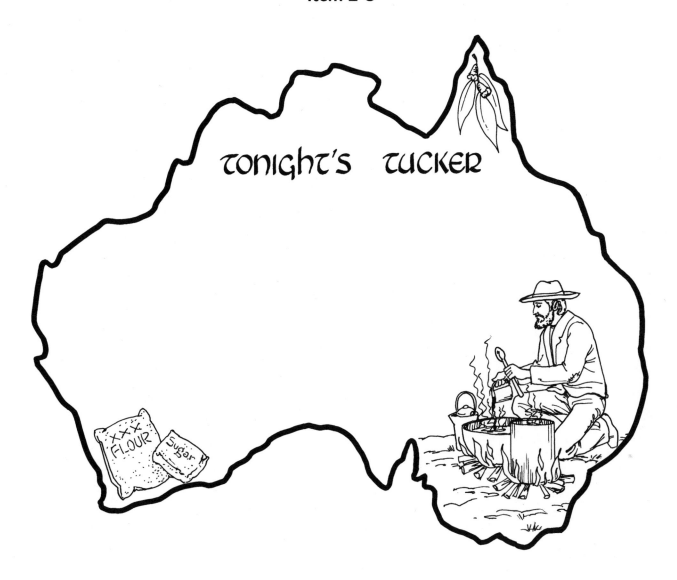

Item 2-P

Pouch

fold

Merit Certificate

_____ Award

Presented to

_____

Date _____

Signed _____

Item 2-T

Item 2-U

Item 3-B

Item 3-C

Single Nest

Item 3-D

Item 3-E

Borrowed
Nest

Uniquely Wonderful

Bibliography

PATCHWORK CHRISTMAS

Boone, Pat. *The Real Christmas.* London: Lakeland Publishers, 1972.

Kailer, Claude, and Rosemary Lowndes. *Make Your Own World of Christmas.* Indianapolis: Bobbs-Merrill, 1972.

Powers, Mala. *Follow the Year.* San Francisco: Harper and Row, 1985.

GIFTS THAT KEEP ON GIVING

Chapin, Alice. *The Big Book of Great Gift Ideas.* Wheaton, Ill.: Tyndale House, 1991.

SCHOOL DAZE

Campbell, Ross. *How to Really Love Your Child.* Wheaton, Ill.: Scripture Press, 1992.

Chapman, Steve and Annie. *Gifts Your Kids Can't Break.* Minneapolis: Bethany House, 1991.

Ortlund, Anne. *Children Are Wet Cement.* Old Tappan, N.J.: Fleming H. Revell, 1981.

Sanders, Bill. *School Daze.* Tarrytown, N.Y.: Fleming H. Revell, 1992.

Smalley, Gary, and John Trent. *The Blessing.* Nashville: Thomas Nelson, 1986.

————. *Building Your Child's Self-esteem.* Colorado Springs: NavPress, 1990.

Zettersten, Rolf. *Train Up a Child.* Dallas: Word, 1991.

FANTASTIC WOMAN

Dengler, Sandy. *Florence Nightingale: Nurse to Soldiers.* Chicago: Moody Press, 1988.

Gosselin, Blanche. "She Hath Done What She Could." *Fundamentalist Journal,* May 1988, 23-27.

Harmon, Rebecca. *Susanna, Mother of the Wesleys.* Nashville: Abingdon Press, 1968.

Karssen, Gien. *Her Name Is Woman.* Colorado Springs: Navpress, 1975.

EVENING IN HOLLAND

Hugget, Frank. *Netherlands: The Land and Its People.* London: Macdonald Educational Holywell House, 1976.

Hunt, Christopher. *Focus on Holland.* London: Hamish Children's Books, 1986.

HIS EYE IS ON THE SPARROW

Emurian, Ernest K. *Forty Stories of Famous Gospel Songs.* Grand Rapids: Baker Book House, 1984.

Mains, Karen B. *Open Heart, Open Home.* Elgin, Ill.: David C. Cook, 1976.

Page, Carol G. *Petals in the Storm.* Ventura, Calif.: Regal Books, 1991.

Reid, J. Calvin. *Birdlife in Wington.* Grand Rapids: William B. Erdmans Publishing Co., 1955.

GOD'S LACE

Billheimer, Paul E. *Don't Waste Your Sorrows.* Minneapolis: Bethany House, 1977.

Foster, Richard J. *Celebration of Discipline.* San Francisco: Harper and Row, 1978.

Lawrence, Brother. *The Practice of the Presence of God.* Grand Rapids: Baker Book House, 1975.

Willard, Dallas. *Spirit of the Disciplines.* San Francisco: Harper and Row, 1988.

Yancey, Phillip. *Disappointment with God.* Grand Rapids: Zondervan Publishing House, 1988.

————. *Where Is God When It Hurts?* Grand Rapids: Zondervan Publishing House, 1990.

UNIQUELY WONDERFUL

Bugbee, Bruce. *Network-Serving Seminar: Equipping Those Who Are Seeking to Serve.* Pasadena, Calif.: Charles E. Fuller Institute, 1989.

Easley, Ken. "Spiritual Gifts: Revealing the Acts of God." *Fulness,* November-December 1982, 2-5.

LaHaye, Tim. *Spirit-controlled Temperament.* Wheaton, Ill.: Tyndale House, 1966.

———. *Transformed Temperaments.* Wheaton, Ill.: Tyndale House, 1971.

McGinn, Linda. *Resource Guide for Women's Ministries.* Nashville: Broadman Press, 1990.

Petro, Sandy. *Discover Your Gift of Fragrance.* Wheaton, Ill.: Scripture Press, 1991.

INDEX